On Nature

Caught by the River
presents

On Nature

Unexpected Ramblings on the British Countryside

Stuart Maconie · Bill Drummond · Tracey Thorn
Martin Noble · Charles Rangeley-Wilson
Chris Yates · Ian Vince · Cheryl Tipp
Ceri Levy · John Wright
And Others

Collins

First published in 2011 by Collins
HarperCollins Publishers
77–85 Fulham Palace Road
London W6 8JB

www.harpercollins.co.uk

15 14 13 12 11
9 8 7 6 5 4 3 2 1

A catalogue record for this book is
available from the British Library

ISBN: 978-0-00-742498-6

Printed and bound in Great Britain by
Clays Ltd, St Ives plc

MIX
Paper from
responsible sources
FSC® C007454

FSC is a non-profit international organisation established to promote the
responsible management of the world's forests. Products carrying the FSC
label are independently certified to assure consumers that they come
from forests that are managed to meet the social, economic and
ecological needs of present and future generations.

Find out more about HarperCollins and the environment at
www.harpercollins.co.uk/green

Contents

Author Biographies   vii
Introduction   xvii

A Chain of Ponds – Chris Yates   1
The Falconer's Tale – Dan Kieran   9
Wainwright Walks – Stuart Maconie   25

How to Tell the Difference between ...
Swallows, Swifts and House Martins   38

Oysteropolis – Michael Smith   41
On the Road to Damascus – Bill Drummond   49
How to Catch Trout – Charles Rangeley-Wilson   61
Name that Tune – Cheryl Tipp   79
Drinking the Seasons – Mark Dredge   85
Reclaiming the Language – Paul Evans   99

How to Tell the Difference between ...
A Primrose and a Cowslip   110

How to See Wildlife – Colin Elford   113
Two Moors Walk – Martin Noble   127
The Night Fisher – Jon Berry   145

How to Bird – Ceri Levy   155
To the Greenhouse – Tracey Thorn   165
Hidden Truth in the Lie of the Land – Ian Vince   177
Deeper than the Wind – Dexter Petley   187
Hush – Robin Turner   199

How to Tell the Difference between ...
        Frogs and Toads   208

Eating the Landscape – John Wright   211
Bracken – Mathew Clayton   235
Winter Pike Fishing – John Andrews   239
The Lazy Naturalist – Nick Small   251
Cycling Round the British Coast – Nick Hand   267

How to Tell the Difference between ...
        Grasshoppers and Crickets   290

Living on a Remote Island – Sarah Boden   293
Radnorshire Annual – Richard King   301
Waterfall Staircase – A. Harry Griffin   313

Author Biographies

Richard Adams

Richard Adams was born in Norfolk, studied Zoology at the University Of Wales, Aberystwyth and can now be found writing about natural history at TheNatureBlog.com

John Andrews

John buys and sells vintage fishing tackle for the soul at a stall in Old Spitalfields market. When not manning the counter, he writes about angling history for Caught by the River, who publish the sporadic Letters from Arcadia (a collaboration with Dexter Petley). He also writes for publications as diverse as *The Times*, *Classic Angling*, the *Old Town Evening Star* and *Waterlog*.

andrewsofarcadia.com

Jon Berry

Jon began fishing at the age of five, catching a tiny trout in a Highland stream. For thirty-five years he has tried to replicate the brilliance of that moment by chasing coarse, game and sea fish in all parts of the British Isles. His first book, *A Can of Worms*, was published in 2007. His follow-up, *Beneath the Black Water*, has recently been published. When not fishing or writing, Jon is a schoolteacher, failed guitarist and supporter of Southampton F.C.

jon-berry.net

Sarah Boden

Sarah is a Hebridean livestock farmer and former assistant editor of the *Observer Music Monthly*.

Mathew Clayton

Mathew lives in Sussex with his wife Gemma and two children Laurie and Stella. He runs Glastonbury Festival's literary area (The Free University of Glastonbury), plays in the Dulwich Ukulele Club and writes and commissions books. In a previous life he commissioned and helped nurture the first Caught by the River book.

Mark Dredge

Mark is an award-winning beer writer who can legitimately say he is working when he goes to the pub. He runs the pencilandspoon.com website. Aged 26 and based in Kent, he is the winner of New Media Beer Writer of the Year 2009/10 from the British Guild of Beer Writers.

pencilandspoon.com

Bill Drummond

Scottish artist Bill Drummond has used various media in his practice including actions, music and words. His actions are too numerous to list, some more infamous than others; his music ranges from the multi-million-selling KLF to the choral music of The17; the words have accumulated into a pile of books.

penkilnburn.com

Colin Elford

Born in Dorset, Colin Elford has watched and studied wildlife his whole life. He has worked as a woodman/deer keeper on a large private estate but for the past twenty years has worked for the Forestry Commission as a forest ranger. He is the author of *A Year in the Woods* (Hamish Hamilton). He has a wife, three children and three grandchildren.

Paul Evans

Paul is a freelance nature writer best known for his country diaries for the *Guardian*; a broadcaster, writing and presenting BBC Radio 4 programmes for the BBC Natural History Unit; and a lecturer in creative writing at Bath Spa University. He has a background in nature conservation and horticulture and a PhD in philosophy. He lives in his native Shropshire with his family.

A. Harry Griffin

A. Harry Griffin was an outdoor man; a climber, a walker and a wanderer. His Country Diary column documented the landscape and community of the Lake District for the *Guardian* and ran uninterrupted for fifty-three years until his death in 2004.

Nick Hand

Bristolian Nick Hand has spent half of his adult life as a graphic designer working without computers and the other half hatching plans to get away from them. He is an enthusiastic city cyclist, married to Harriet, and has three grown-up children.

slowcoast.co.uk

Dan Kieran

Dan is an author and co-founder of the crowd-funding publishing platform Unbound. He has written and edited nine books including *Crap Towns*, *I Fought the Law* and *Three Men in a Float*. He contributes to the *Guardian*, *The Times*, the *Observer*, the *Telegraph* and the *Idler*.

dankieran.com

Richard King

Richard King lives in Radnorshire and is the editor of *Loops*. His book *How Soon is Now*, the inside history of the independent music industry 1975–2005 will be published by Faber & Faber in 2012.

Ceri Levy

Ceri is a documentary filmmaker, writer and producer best known for the documentary film *Bananaz* about the band Gorillaz. Ceri is at present working on a film about the way birds inspire and affect people called *The Bird Effect*.

thebirdeffect.com

Stuart Maconie

Stuart is a TV and radio presenter, journalist, columnist and author. His much-loved book *Pies and Prejudice* has been one of the publishing successes of recent years and *Adventures On The High Teas* was the bestselling travel book of 2010. His books have been translated into Japanese, Russian, Italian and German. He co-hosts the 'Radcliffe and Maconie Show' on BBC 6 Music and presides over the same station's genre-defying *Freak Zone*.

stuartmaconie.com

Martin Noble

Martin is the lead guitarist with Britain's premier rock'n'roll outdoorsmen, British Sea Power. A keen birdwatcher, Martin contributed to the celebrated BBC radio documentary *In Search of the Holy Quail*.

britishseapower.co.uk

Dexter Petley

Dexter was born in the Weald of Kent and now lives in a yurt in France. He is a novelist, translator, angling writer as well as a radical anti-social surviving on low energy, permaculture and mushroom gathering.

dexterpetley.com

Charles Rangeley-Wilson

Charles is an angler and writer and photographer. His work regularly appears in the *Telegraph*, *The Times*, the *Independent* and the *Guardian*. His first book, *Somewhere Else*, was shortlisted for the WHSmith Sports Book of the Year. Its sequel, *The Accidental Angler*, was AWA Travel Book of the Year and a successful BBC series. His next book – the history of a river – is due for publication in 2012 by Random House.

charlesrangeley-wilson.com

Nick Small

Nick is a film fettlin', music video meddlin', photography peddlin', bilberry pickin', boreal forest dwellin', wild river lovin' man o' the North.

Michael Smith

Michael Smith is the author of *The Giro Playboy* and *Shorty Loves Wing Wong*. He appears regularly on *The Culture Show* and has made various documentaries for the BBC. He lives and works in London but tries to get away to his beach hut as often as he can.

michaelsmithwordsandfilms.com

Tracey Thorn

After an eighteen-year career with partner Ben Watt as Everything but the Girl, Tracey went on a self-imposed hiatus to start a family. Since re-emerging in 2007 she has released two critically acclaimed solo albums (*Out of the Woods* and *Love and its Opposite*). Tracey is Caught by the River's gardening correspondent.

traceythorn.com

Cheryl Tipp

Cheryl is curator of the wildlife sounds collection at the British Library. She graduated from Queen Mary, University of London, in 2000 with a First Class degree in Zoology. Previous publications include *Sounds of the British Coastline*, *Secret Songs of Birds* and *Beautiful Bird Songs of Britain*.

Robin Turner

Robin is one third of Caught by the River. He co-authored the *Rough Pub Guide* and conceived and ran Roam, an art project in a disused mobile library that took place across east London in 2010. Although he never stops rattling on about Wales and Welshness, he lives happily in Hackney with his fiancée, his daughter Pip and their cat Honey.

robinturnerwriting.wordpress.com

Ian Vince

Ian is the author of five non-fiction books including his latest, *The Lie of the Land*, an under-the-field guide to the British landscape. An erstwhile columnist, editor and failed scriptwriter, he lives in Salisbury with his wife and two children.

britishlandscape.org

John Wright

John Wright lives with his wife and two teenage daughters in rural Dorset. Having followed his private passion for foraging fungi and wild plants, he has become a regular contributor to the *River Cottage* programme as well as many other TV shows. He also runs wild food forays in his local area. John has written several books in the River Cottage series and has three future titles in the pipeline.

wild-food.net

Chris Yates

If there's one person who epitomises the ethos behind Caught by the River, it's probably Chris Yates. Angler, author, tea connoisseur, Chris is perfect company, a mellow-as-you-like raconteur and all-round inspiration. His books (*Casting at the Sun*, *How to Fish* and *Out of the Blue*) and his TV shows (*A Passion for Angling*) are classics – for both those who fish and those not yet hooked. His next book is due this year.

Introduction

How can you get the most out of Britain? Although a strange question, it was one we at Caught by the River found ourselves asking. We wondered – after having immersed ourselves in the great modern chroniclers of the countryside such as Deakin, Yates, Macfarlane and Mabey – how you could apply the subtle magic of their books to your life. You might love great angling writing but how do you actually read water? You know the blue tit from the blackbird in your back garden but what's the best way to start birding? What's edible and growing freely in your local area? And how on earth do you do the Wainwright Walk?

With those questions in mind, we were inspired to answer them in a book. *On Nature* – the follow-up to our previous collection, *Words on Water* – would be a 'How To' guide to the British Isles, written by the people who understood the landscape the best. We asked a list of Caught by the River contributors (and a fair few people whose work we admired but had never met before) if they were interested in writing about their particular field of interest. The book would be a beautifully written user's guide to our country. From foraging to fly fishing, birding to brewing, *On Nature* would offer pointers, primers and pertinent lessons from those in the know, passing knowledge to those willing to learn.

Well, that's how we thought it would end up.

When Bill Drummond wrote to us and pledged to write a piece on the importance of damsons, we knew that our original brief was being abandoned. In the hands of people like Bill, our 'How To' guide soon became something very, very different. Before long we were looking at a kaleidoscopic vision of Britain, one where writers talked about their connection to the land in a series of stories that would hopefully inspire action. Here, life on remote islands was not only possible, it was desirable. Watching the seasons change through a Welsh kitchen window took on the elemental lyrical ebb and flow of an R.S. Thomas poem. Angling stories became boy's own adventures; falconry an obvious pastime for day-dreaming urban naturalists.

Looking at the finished article, *On Nature* is a collection of stories highlighting the kind of uncontrollable driving forces that get people up at 4 a.m. to cast off in the half-light, or to go mushroom hunting in dewy meadows. It's about watching and listening, digging in, taking part. It's about people's passions for the countryside – the kind that start out as hobbies before turning into unshakable obsessions.

Charles Rangeley-Wilson summed it up perfectly in his contribution on trout fishing. To quote him, '*I wonder then if the best way of describing* the how *is to start at the beginning with* the why: *if at the beginning of the how there is a passion – encompassing all the associated meanings of that word: desire, compulsion, infatuation – once found it will guide the rest of the discovery. With passion in your tackle bag the how will ultimately take care of itself.'*

So, whether using tackle bag or train ticket, a pair of binoculars or just a pair of ears, *On Nature* maps Britain in sights, sounds and subtle memories, offering jumping-in points and inspirations for eager urban naturalists everywhere.

Just remember to pack an open mind.

Jeff, Andrew and Robin
Caught by the River, Spring 2011

A Chain of Ponds

Chris Yates

In the 1950s the old village of Burgh Heath, which was my childhood home, used to be a hotchpotch of unremarkable 18th- and 19th-century cottages, with two pubs, a cobbler's, corn stores, stables, sweet shop and tea gardens. Surrounding the village was an area of heathland – perfect ground for every kind of childhood game – and lapping the tea gardens was the pond, an acre of greenish water that, by the time I was five, was the centre of my universe.

No normal child can resist water, and because post-war parents did not live in constant fear for their children's lives I could spend countless summer days either on my own or with friends playing on the bankside. In the beginning I was ignorant of anything that might possibly have lived beneath the surface; I only wanted to throw stones and make as big a splash as possible. I soon learnt, though, that if there was an angler on the bank it was best not to throw anything; anglers could get quite cross if I even splashed my feet near them. This was understandable once they explained the necessity for quiet. Their stories intrigued me and added a completely new dimension to the world, but did the fabulous-sounding creatures they described truly exist? In those early days I never saw a fisherman catch anything, and when I began to creep around the margins, peering expectantly into the green depths, I spotted nothing more exciting than watersnails, tadpoles and leeches. Perhaps fishing was just an adult form of make-believe, though at least it gave a person an excuse to sit happily by the waterside for hours on end, doing nothing.

My three best friends, Billy, Colin and Dennis, were just as enthusiastic about the pond as I was, yet all they ever wanted to do was sail their model boats. I would, of course, accompany them on regatta days, launching various craft that in former times had only plied across the bath at home. My pals had yachts with proper cotton sails while I had a wooden canoe with two Apache Indians and – my pride and joy – a clockwork rowing boat with a man who rocked back and forth as he pulled on the oars. One memorable day, when the motor was fully wound, he rowed as far as the island in the pond's centre, but, as we were waiting for the breeze to waft him back to shore, a stone came whistling out of the sky and almost capsized him.

On the opposite bank a gang of unknown boys maybe twice our age were collecting pebbles prior to the destruction of our fleet by catapults. Of my friends, only Dennis possessed such a weapon, and on that day it was not in his pocket. However, had we all been armed we would not have been so daft as to return fire against such murderously superior opposition. Our only hope lay in the fact that we were on the heathland side where there was plenty of cover, if only we could gather the drifting fleet in time. We swamped our boots, there were a few more near misses, yet we retrieved our craft and escaped without serious injury. Following a narrow twisting path that led through man-high bracken, we ran towards a distant wood. The sound of our fleeing was like the sound of cavalry galloping across a shallow ford; even when we reached the trees our boots were still half filled with pondwater. The enemy had pursued us, but we had been quick enough, vanishing into the ferns before they had even circuited the pond. Now we pushed deeper into the wood until we found a quiet place to sit a moment, draw breath and drain our wellingtons.

It seemed sensible that we should circle round, keeping under the trees as far as the Reigate Road which would lead us safely home. However, after just a few yards we saw the unexpected glitter of water through the shadows and, turning from our intended path, came upon another pond. It was a quarter the size of the village pond, saucer-shaped and surrounded by tall reeds. The water looked deep and crystal clear and it was obvious we had made an important, magical discovery. Not wanting to linger too long, we turned again and followed a track leading between thickets of blackthorn to the new pond's almost identical twin. Once more, we dared not pause and savour it for long, but made sure we'd remember the way back for a future exploration. Continuing along the path we stumbled on yet another tiny reed-encircled pool. It lay just beyond the last line of trees on the edge of a wide grassy field, and because it seemed so far from the known world, so impossible for anyone else to discover, we felt safe enough to crawl under a wire fence, step out into the sunlight and sit by the water.

For a few minutes we kept hold of our model boats, but the complete quiet reassured us and we put them down, though no one was bold enough to refloat them, nor, I think, did we even consider this: it was enough simply to have escaped persecution and fled into this foreign and enchanted field. It stretched down a long gentle incline towards an incredibly distant horizon of blueish pine trees. Over to our left a derelict barn leaned out of a clump of trees, beyond which a group of cows were lying in the shade of a solitary elm. Dennis, who was not looking at the view, suddenly shouted 'Newt!' very loudly and made me jump. He pointed down into the pond where a golden finger-length creature was hanging motionless in the water with its nose poking up through the surface. Its feet were spread like tiny hands and the dark crest along the length of its back and tail gave it the appearance of a miniature dinosaur. It blew a single bubble, turned slowly and with a flick vanished into the glassy depth.

Unlike Dennis, I had never seen a newt before, yet even he seemed excited. All four of us crept round the spongy bank, looking for another, hoping to capture it and maybe bring it home in a wet sock. Though the water was perfectly transparent – so different from the cloudy village pond – and though I spotted a monster water beetle (which I only later discovered was a dragonfly larva), there were no more amphibians on display. Perhaps if we returned for a whole day with one of the little nets they sold in the corn stores we might be more successful, but only Dennis and I wanted the hunt to become more serious.

Safely back home, I looked through all my picture books for an illustration of a newt. Naturally there were dragons and sea monsters and dinosaurs, but I could not find any newts until my helpful elder sister, Helen, tracked one down in her Children's Encyclopedia. It was not quite as impressive as the real thing, yet it kept me happy and inspired until the day came when Dennis and I journeyed back to the field pond. We did not call in at the corn stores on the way and buy a net: there was no need as Dennis's big brother had described an alternative and far more effective method of newting. All we needed, he said, was a long thin stick, two yards of button thread and some worms. Apparently, this had been a long-held elder brother's secret, but now he was taken up with other passions he could finally reveal it.

With our newt rods and our lines baited with a knotted-on worm we looked like a couple of genuine anglers. It was so thrilling I could hardly speak, though I was not certain, despite what Dennis's brother had told us, what would happen if a newt actually grabbed the bait. Would I be able to tell? Would it hang on long enough to be swung ashore? Maybe five or twenty-five long minutes passed before Dennis pointed nervously at his twitching line. I probably gasped as he snatched it up – but there was nothing there – not even the worm. Something had stolen it all. As Dennis rebaited, my line quivered where it slanted through the surface. I immediately flicked it into the air where, like a miracle, a fantastic creature suddenly appeared, hands spread out, swinging towards me. Only when it was on the grass next to me did it let go of the worm.

Reverently, I picked it up and held it in the palm of my hand. Its quiet eyes and slow careful movements helped calm me down a little, but my heart kept pounding because, at that moment, my newt – olive green with webbed hind claws, a palmate newt – was the most wondrous thing I had ever seen. And with it swimming in a jam-jar I could take it home and say I had caught more than the fishermen.

The Falconer's Tale

Dan Kieran

For most of us the countryside is a realm of escape; a living postcard that runs in real time through your brain, somewhere to dream of when you are immersed in the mania of a city. A walk in this landscape loosens your shoulders and draws out your breath in soft gasps. Waves 'dance', flowers 'flutter' and the promise of lusty milkmaids is only ever the next valley away. This is nature in soft focus, the Wordsworthian idyll of our imagination where we carelessly love to play.

Stalking through the woods with a hawk on your gloved fist strips nature of such romance but keeps its authenticity vividly intact. The memory of something more agile and real about the living, wild world begins to seep out of your bones and your focus razors. His head moves slowly and methodically, the wings stretch out as he rebalances with his yellow taloned feet and the eyes flit and twitch. No longer passively consuming the landscape from the audience, he pulls you onto the stage. The breeze flattens. Birdsong scatters. Silence. The sound of the wild food chain. You begin to feel the pressure of every living thing in the earth on the back of your neck as you pace beyond the gorse, but even in this heightened state you are ponderous. Remaining sure-footed, his head plunges towards the ground, anticipating a vole's movement, but by the time your gaze lands with his you are lucky to glimpse a shoe-lace tail vanish into the grass. Your shoulders broaden with anticipation and you untie the falconer's knot that binds him to your glove with your right hand and lightly hold the jesses – the soft leather straps attached to his ankles – between the fingers and palm of your left. Hawks and falcons calculate unconsciously whether the energy required to catch potential quarry is worth the effort. You think of the astonishing triangulation these instincts perform when a flurry of feathers brushes your face. You instinctively open your hand, extend your arm and reel slightly. He's off – coursing through the light.

This sensation of closeness between tamed man and wild bird has a lineage that goes back millennia. According to the written, or more often drawn, archive that we use to trace the route of history, hawks and falcons were first used to hunt for food in China and Mesopotamia around 700 BC. From the training to the equipment it requires, the essential elements of falconry are unchanged since that time. Practised by emperors, soldiers, commoners and men and women, falconry, or hawking, crossed the deserts of Asia, the Middle East and Africa before conquering the disparate realms of Europe and the New World. The practice graces the oral poetry and written pages of ancient texts in every culture it has touched along the way, popping up in the writings and stories of kings and emperors (most notably Emperor Frederick II, 1194–1250), a Tsar (Alexei Romanov, 1629–76), an Arabic astronomer (*The Book of Moamyn*, *c.*1200), Saxon poetry ('The Battle of Maldon', 991), our own Knights of the Round Table (Sir Tristan is a renowned harpist and falconer), monks (*The Boke of St Albans*, 1486) and, perhaps most exotically for a Western mind, in those of the warriors of the Samurai (*Nihon Shoki*, the *Chronicles of Japan*, 720). To learn that the feeling of setting out with a hawk on your fist in the hunt for food, partnering with a bird's natural wild behaviour, is something that has been experienced by such varied ancestors adds a glint of substance to the myth of their forgotten lives. I like to think their shadows drift with you in the woods – the echo of a collective experience ingrained in our very species.

What the Samurai or the Knights of the Round Table would have made of my initial experience of falconry is harder to imagine. The first time a Harris hawk landed on my fist I was standing in the rain in the middle of a pine forest surrounded by wooden lodges in the dystopian eco-habitat of Center Parcs in Somerset as part of a group of seven people clad in bright waterproofs with arms outstretched, as a hawk did its duty and flew from the falconer to each of us in turn. But despite my location and the formulaic atmosphere, experiencing a wild bird fly towards me for the first time – so I could see exactly how the tail feathers push the air to slow the hawk to the point that it can literally step from flight onto my fist – was surely little different to the sensation it must have evoked for the first time in a squire in medieval England or a warrior in Jomon Japan. This was a spectacle, biology, sport, instinct, a privileged insight into wild behaviour and a philosophy of life all merged into one. In the ten years since that experience I have become an avid fan of hawks and falcons. I've gone on falconry experience days and holidays and read every obscure book on the subject I can trace. I've had barn owls, eagle owls, kestrels, lanner and peregrine falcons, all kinds of hybrids, a merlin and even a golden eagle perched on my fist. I drove for six hours one Saturday morning to the edge of Cornwall from Sussex with my friend Kev once – just on the off chance we might glimpse a snowy owl that had got lost on migration.

But while I love raptors in all their forms Harris hawks have always been my favourite. Known as the 'wolves of the air' because of their habit of hunting in packs of up to six, they are highly social, have the ideal temperament for falconry and a hunting style most accommodating to human beings. Their natural habitat is desert where one of them will scout ahead, others will walk along the ground in the hope of scaring something into movement, while those that remain wait above – preparing to strike. The group then share whatever is caught. Going hunting with Harris hawks is certainly the most self-contained, dramatic, inspiring and shocking thing I have ever done.

It's important to appreciate that a trained hawk or falcon of any kind bears absolutely no relation to a domesticated pet. Birds of prey only remain with the falconer as long as he or she remains a more efficient food source than the bird could achieve out in the wild. It's a relationship but by no means a friendship. Even if a hawk or falcon consented to remain with you for twenty years their wild instincts would remain intact. This is why the jesses are made from leather, or sometimes kangaroo skin, because eventually they will rot and fall off should the falcon one day decide it has had enough of you. Everything about the husbandry involved in taking care of a hawk is based with transience in mind. This is as true for a falconry enthusiast in the UK as it is for those who still rely on birds of prey for food and animal skins in the mountains of Kazakhstan. Go there today and you'll still find men and their sons hawking on horseback with golden eagles on the fist. Sixteen-year-old boys are sent down a cliff face with simple rope to take a juvenile eagle from its eyrie. They train them for six months under the watchful eye of their fathers and then hunt with them for nine years. After that they release them, grateful for the work they have done (golden eagles can live over thirty years in the wild and up to eighty in captivity).

Despite often being bundled up with other country sports, falconry is also far more awesome and has little in common with fox hunting, or shooting pheasants or deer.

Instead of stacking the odds in your favour with technology or superior numbers you participate in natural behaviour to catch your prey. It might seem a little blood curdling, but I'd rather be a wild rabbit and take my chances with a Harris hawk than a chicken in a battery farm. As for enjoying the act of death? Well, to be honest, that's my least favourite part but I'm of the view that if you can't bring yourself to kill an animal then you have no right to eat it. Not that the food argument is relevant from a human perspective anyway. Whenever I've been hunting with Harris hawks they've been catching their own dinner.

Back in the woods he's gone. Blending through a thicket of trees. The possibility of a squirrel or a resting bird perhaps. You hear the bell on his ankle tinkling and follow the sound, jogging and ducking through the branches. Cautious, you feel the eyes around you as the bracken folds under your feet. Then through the damp, newly fallen leaves suddenly the bell is louder. You spot him standing atop a tree, looking around with feathers rousing about his neck. His vision is tunnelled, seeking prey. You try and call yourself into his mind, tapping a scrap of meat on your left thumb with your right hand. He spots it instantly and embraces the air. His wings are flat but his head tilts, almost with curiosity, and he glides towards you. Minimum effort, maximum effect. From that vantage point he swoops below the line of your fist before adjusting and rising up again. The wings open, his powerful feet thrust forward and tail feathers break the air. Feet on flesh but with barely any sensation of impact. You grin broadly. His beak immediately pulls at the food on your hand and you tuck the jesses between your thumb and finger. Finished, he opens his wings to adjust and looks ahead. Concentrating. Still hungry. Looking for something else.

Becoming a falconer is not something to attempt on a whim. The training and hard work required is seldom appreciated by the hawk, but the most important factor is time. That's why, for most serious falconers to do it properly, they have to be absurdly rich, unmarried and have no children, or they have to make falconry earn them a living. Being in the company of a falconer who has made it their career is always inspiring. It is hard work, with astonishingly long hours, but certainly not a mundane job. They enthuse and cajole newcomers by sharing their birds and their enthusiasm but offer plenty of stories of warning and danger too. They have no time for people who embark on the process of having a wild bird if they are not prepared to show the bird the respect required by learning how to care for it properly. In the UK today you don't need a licence to have a bird of prey and no one comes to check if you're housing it properly – even though these are wild and dangerous birds. A warm and gentle falconer I spent a few days with in Scotland once told me a story about a novice who took it upon himself to get a golden eagle as his first bird. This man was as mild a soul as I have ever met but he almost delighted in telling me how the novice failed to show the eagle the necessary respect and the precise details of how he was consequently attacked, losing the sight in one eye in the process. People are normally uneasy about having a bird of prey on their fist because they're afraid of the bird's beak, but it's little more than a knife and fork. The taloned feet are what you have to watch out for. Only an arrogant fool or a respectful master of falconry would dare to offer a home to a golden eagle.

The woods clear and you climb a small hill, where the tufts and clumps of grass shelter rabbit holes. As you reach the top a long shallow valley falls away towards a derelict barn and a lonely telegraph pole. He bates, feathers wildly flapping, and fights to be free of your fist. With the height you've gained he wants to claim the roof of the barn. Now. Then you'll walk towards him and scare the quarry as you come. He can sit, wait and pounce. Simple. You want him to work a little harder than that. You scoop him up and back on to your fist. He screams violence in your face, but any eye contact is unconscious. You walk gingerly through the holes along the ridge, heading further on.

The annals of falconry offer a variety of methods for training your bird, a process that begins with 'manning'. You have to grind down the bird's natural instincts to flee from you by keeping him on your fist for as long as possible. Eventually he will accept you, and when he is hungry enough will drop his eyes and eat from your fist. This is the first step in training the bird. Feeding from the fist opens up the possibilities of more advanced training as he begins to associate you with food. In *The Goshawk*, T.H. White struggles with the tempestuous Gos, who is delivered from

Germany in a basket, only a few weeks old and still never
having seen another living thing:

> ... he was tumultuous and frightening ... born to fly, sloping
> sideways, free among the verdure of that Teutonic upland, to
> murder with his fierce feet and to consume with that curved
> Persian beak, who now hopped up and down in a clothes
> basket with a kind of imperious precocity, the impatience of
> a spoiled but noble heir-apparent to the Holy Roman
> Empire.

White introduces himself to Gos in a barn, and what follows
is a battle of patience and instinct as White attempts to force
Gos to accept him. Endlessly placing him on his fist only for
Gos to 'bate' and end up suspended by his jesses until White
again puts him on his fist, and on it goes.

> I was to stay awake if necessary for three days and nights,
> during which, I hoped, the tyrant would learn to stop his
> bating and to accept my hand as a perch, would consent to
> eat there, and would become a little accustomed to the
> strange life of human beings.

Eventually Gos accepts White, suffering to sit on his fist
while he walks around his farm, into town and even on a
visit to the local pub.

Happily these days the best method of training birds of
prey is more widely agreed on and much less stressful for

both bird and man. For one thing eggs are no longer taken from nests but laid in captivity, and chicks are fed from the glove from the moment they hatch. This 'imprints' the person doing the feeding as the parent and means the bird will accept food from anyone from that moment on – as long as it is offered from a glove. This process makes the hawk or falcon think that you and they are the same species. While this has obvious benefits when it comes to training, it also means that they have no fear of you and if cornered will attack. Falconers also introduce the 'lure' earlier in the training process these days too. Feeding a bird of prey from a small leather pouch at the end of a long string familiarises the bird with the lure as a food source. You can then drag the lure, with food and/or animal fur attached, to 'remind' the bird of its natural behaviour when the bird is more mature. Because they tend to hunt prey that lives on the ground, hawks and eagles are taught to go for a dragged lure to simulate chasing rabbits and small animals. Falcons will hunt other birds on the wing (in mid air). In this instance the bird, familiar with the lure as a food source, will attempt to catch the lure when the falconer swings it around his head. Expert lure practitioners strengthen their falcons and improve their hunting ability by sweeping the lure away at the last minute in a cross between a choreographed dance and a martial art. (I've tried my hand at lure swinging, but was no match for the saker falcon I found myself pitted against. She mugged me for it on her first attempt.) The falcon needs this kind of training so it can cope with hunting in the wild – I saw a hobby hunting bats at dusk on the River Avon once, which was stupefying. Falcons have an instinctive agility that the human eye can barely match, but as the falconer is aiming to push the falcon into discovering its innate ability rather than teach it everything from scratch, it doesn't take long for the bird to 'get it' and successfully hunt on its own.

The ridge softens and you stop in front of a bramble bush that shelters you from the field, slowly untying the falconer's knot and releasing the jesses with your right hand. Closer to the barn now, you raise your arm and push him into the air. You must not let him get too far away. He glides down towards the roof, and lands on its highest point. You are 100 metres or so away when you begin to walk towards the barn. The brown fur of a rabbit lollops near you, but he just sits – it's not worth it. He looks behind the barn, spots something and vanishes. Damn! But you don't run. There's no point. You twinge in panic – could this be the day he decides to leave? It's always possible, but no. You remember his hunting weight. It's just hunger driving instinct. Then he reappears on the roof. You relax with relief. You start to move again. The wave of impact from your footsteps begins to interest him, he spots something but there's no movement. Then he beats his wings and dives down. The rabbit that you can't see has a fifty-fifty chance. You imagine it darting left and right, heading for a hole. The hawk seems to be going too slowly. He's barely moving his wings, then he arcs one way and then another. You see it! The rabbit's back legs force him into a high leap over something, towards a bush. Then he stoops, wings raised and feet falling, covering, and then there's no sound. You run now, forgetting the holes. You charge and find them both. He turns to you and squawks mercilessly. The rabbit is alive, one eye fixed in terror and the heart juddering under its fur. He mantles with his wings, talons gripping the rabbit's face and back. Not sharing, not yet. You offer something else from the bag, a whole chick that's dead – easier to eat and no risk of injury. Your left hand now firmly presses down on the rabbit's back. He jumps for the chick and eats it in one go, cocking his neck to swallow. Your right hand reaches for the rabbit's neck. You pause, registering the soft fur, and then you pull hard. The rabbit's neck breaks and the fight is gone. You feel exhilarated and shocked. The quarry goes into your bag.

You sit in the wet grass. Breathless. He stands on the floor. There is no pleasure in death but also no regret. His eyes flit and twitch. You are tame. He is wild. This is the world. A glimpse of the truth that lies behind every breath becomes clearer in the cold autumn light. Whether you would have it or not, this is the world. Climbing to your feet you hold out your fist. He flaps his wings impatiently and is up. His feet tangle with the jesses. You unravel them and hold them between the fingers and palm of your left hand. He's still concentrating. Still hungry. Always looking for something else.

Recommended reading:
   The Goshawk by T.H. White
   Falconry by Emma Ford
   A Manual of Falconry by M.H. Woodford
   England Have My Bones by T.H. White

Selection of falconry terms (reprinted from Harting's
Bibliotheca Accipitraria*):*
   AYRE and EYRIE, nesting place. 'Our *aiery* buildeth
      in the cedar's top.' – Shakespeare.
   BATE, BATING, fluttering or flying off the fist. 'It is
      calde batyng for she batith with hirselfe, most oftyn
      causeless.' – *Boke of St Albans*, 1486.
   BOWSE, to drink; variously spelt 'bouse', 'boose',
      'bouze' and 'booze'.
   CADGER, the person who carries the hawk; hence
      the abbreviated form 'cad', a person fit for no other
      occupation.
   LURE, technically a bunch of feathers or couple of
      wings tied together on a piece of leather and
      weighted.
   MANNING, making a hawk tame by accustoming
      her to man's presence.
   MEWS, the place where hawks are set down to
      moult.
   QUARRY, the game flown at.
   ROUSE, when 'a hawk lifteth herself up and shaketh
      herself' – *Boke of St Albans*, 1486.

STOOP, the swift descent of a falcon on the quarry
from a height.

Recommended falconry courses:
British School of Falconry, Gleneagles, Scotland:
www.gleneagles.com.
Frontline Falconry, Auchen Castle, Scotland: www.
auchencastle.net; www.frontlinefalconry.co.uk.

Wainwright Walks

Stuart Maconie

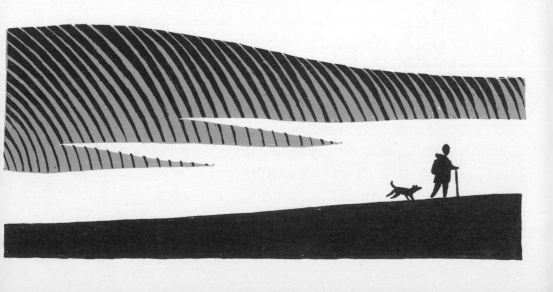

On the front of the first edition of a book of mine called *Cider with Roadies*, there's a picture I love. It's taken in a nightclub called Bluto's in Wigan in about 1978 and it's of me and my teenage friend Dylan. He looks like trouble, frankly. You would cross the road to avoid him with his toothless snarling visage, however hammed up for the camera. I am looking, well, like a bit of a ponce actually. I'm in the grip of my adolescent Elvis Costello fixation and am wearing a grey '50s demob-style jacket, a white bri-nylon shirt and a blue knitted tie. So far, so hipster. But my hair is all wrong and my glasses are not Costello nerd chic but tinted Doobie Brothers 'style'. In time I would grow to love the Doobie Brothers but that time would not be for another decade at least. On the streets of Wigan in 1978 we cool kids aspired to Camden, not California.

I have another favourite picture of Dylan and me (he was named after Dylan Thomas, loved the Clash and Kate Bush and, slightly disappointingly, became a policeman, but if you're reading this, mate, I hope you're well). In this one we are dressed very similarly – me in a leather bomber jacket, bumpers, Beatlecut and fag, I seem to have transferred my allegiance to Colin Moulding of XTX, whilst Dylan wears his shitstopper jeans and Clash T-shirt, but we are al fresco. By Esthwaite Water in the Lake District, looking distinctly pleased with ourselves as we cradle a plump olive-green tench in our muddy hands. A good six pounds, I'd say, which was very good for us.

Though we were resolutely urban kids – the telly went straight off in our house when Jack Hargreaves came on, droning on about horse brasses and silage – our nocturnal pursuit of fun ran completely and happily parallel to a kind of punk Tom Sawyer existence of fishing and camping. We would often pile straight into Joe Mather's dad's van and go straight from a nightclub to a local canal or flash or gravel pit and spend the dawn catching nothing but talking about girls and listening to Radio One on the transistor radio before falling asleep in the morning sun and waking two hours later bitten to death, sunburned and starving.

Mostly, though, we loved to head up the M6 to the Lake District for a weekend, usually spent catching a few fish and absolutely no girls. No matter. We had fun drinking in the pubs of Hawkshead by evening and poaching eels from the lakes overnight under cover of darkness, girded by seven pints of Jennings Cumberland Ales. The poaching of eels was a highly skilled and technical endeavour undertaken with as much ruthless efficiency as a teenage boy can when he's drunk his own body weight in bitter, and eel fishing is very exciting. An eel is, in its purest essence, a thick muscular inner tube with a primitive central nervous system. They give you a hell of a fight and they taste kind of nutty. We ate them for breakfast every morning, cooked up on the old Primus stove at Farmer Brass's campsite in the oddest and often least palatable combinations: eel risotto, eel kedgeree, eel au vin, vegetable curry with eelao rice, spaghetti eelanaise. Eventually I came to fantasise about one dark night being lucky enough to pull a Variety pack of sugar puffs or a Heinz Toast Topper from the murky depths, anything that meant I wouldn't have to have bloody eels again.

And on most of these trips, an item or two from Dylan's bookshelf would accompany us. Not one of Richard Allen's New English Library Suedehead thug fests. Not the well-thumbed NME *Book of Rock* – the one with the controversial verdict on Jethro Tull's *Minstrel in the Gallery*. No. One of a series of volumes that I'd noticed as soon as I'd first set foot in Dylan's house. His dad was an English teacher – hence the Dylan Thomas fixation – and he had all kinds of cool stuff, Kerouac, Mailer, *The Gulag Archipelago*. But my eye had been drawn to six or seven little hardback books that were obviously some kind of series. One was brown, another yellow, another green. They were hand-written and hand-drawn, things of such painstaking elegance of design and craft that even though the subject – Cumbrian hills – didn't much appeal, the sheer loveliness of them, plus the maps and the local info, made them treasurable. They seemed to be written by a bloke called Wainwright. I imagined he was a bit of an anorak.

Three decades on and on the shelf beside me are not one but two full sets of Alfred Wainwright's *Seven Volume Pictorial Guide to the Lake District Fells*. Look closely at the two sets and you'll notice a crucial difference that explains the need for both. One set is battered and dog-eared, stained with coffee and smeared with butter, stained with grass and dirt. The other is relatively pristine, the reason being that one is for the fireside and the other for the fellside, one sees action in the field, the other nothing more strenuous than being pored over whilst planning a day's adventures.

Notwithstanding the disadvantage of being dead, Alfred Wainwright has had a good few years of late. There've been biographies and celebrations. There's a society bearing his name. And thanks to the *Wainwright Walks* TV series, a new generation has been inspired to take to the hills and retrace the steps he walked in between the late 1950s and the mid 1960s when researching his famous guide books. The success of the shows was due in no small measure to the choice of presenter, the extremely personable Julia Bradbury, a refreshing choice after years of blokes from the Jack Hargreaves school of outdoors TV presentation – crusty, bearded, curmudgeonly.

All of which could be said to apply to Wainwright himself, or at least that's the popular image. But he had his poetic side, one that drew him from the dark satanic mills of his native Blackburn to Kendal to be nearer his beloved hills. He'd have approved of Julia too. AW was a sucker for a pretty face. He was more than just that, in fact; he was a true romantic. His love letters to his second wife, Betty, are mildly shocking in their intensity and tenderness, especially if you had him tagged as a harrumphing sourpuss. But if you know the books, you'll know his lyrical and poetic side too. That's the side that has made millions like me a devotee of his work, even when it was a love that dare not speak its name, such as during my tenure as an *NME* writer, when a liking for anything more outdoorsy than the healing field at Glastonbury marked you out as a weirdo amongst weirdos.

Wainwright classified 214 separate fells as making up the mountain landscape of the Lake District. Pedants and purists grumble about his list, saying that some such as Mungrisedale Common – a grassy pudding beneath the infinitely superior rocky throne of Blencathra – is not a separate fell at all and that Wainwright included it just to make up the numbers in book 6. This may be true. But now the list is canonical, and there are folk who will not rest until they have crested the summit of every one. I know because I am one. I'm not one of nature's list tickers – I don't collect records, I don't keep a diary – but I decided to 'do the Wainwrights' as it would be a ready-made itinerary that would take me to every corner of the Lake District. It has been a long, strange, brilliant trip, to paraphrase the Grateful Dead.

It has taught me loads about myself and others. It has made me laugh and cry; given me a treasure house of memories to be endlessly raided.

So where do you start? Go to the original volumes. There are any number of interpretations, re-workings, spins and spin-offs, but no one has improved on AW's original pen and ink works. The artwork is gorgeous, the writing hugely quirky and characterful as well as evocative. And though the occasional right of way may have changed, the mountains don't. With decent gear, a 1:25,000 OS Map and the relevant Wainwright, you should be able to tackle any of the 214 Wainwrights even if you don't have a beard. Wainwright was adventurous, but he was never foolhardy. He always has a word of sound advice for the novice fellwalker.

Of course, that advice can sometimes be quite, shall we say, bracing. There I was, by the unnamed rocky pool that hangs pendant as a teardrop on the jagged, awkward, thoroughly delicious top of Haystacks. I was that novice and had rather bitten off more mountain than I could chew. Having got a couple of fells under my belt and loved the exhilaration and atmosphere of the high places, I'd volunteered to take a mixed group of 'newbies' – kids, dogs, couples, skinny, plump, all kagouled and rucksacked – to the top of the justly famous Haystacks. I was confidence itself at first. We were well shod, buttied and flasked, I had a map and my freshly purchased copy of Volume 6 (the yellow one). Haystacks, unlike the '70s wrestler of the same name, is no giant. But it is glorious. Wainwright says of it that 'it stands unabashed … in the midst of a circle of much loftier hills, like a shaggy terrier in the company of foxhounds … but not one of this distinguished group of mountains … can show a greater variety and a more fascinating arrangement of interesting features'.

Shaggy, fascinating, yes, all these things. But disconcerting, too on that afternoon. For as we reached the summit a thick, drenching shroud of hill fog, 'clag' as the mountaineers call it, came in from the Cumbrian coast, and suddenly, where once there had been familiar landmarks and unmistakable paths, there was a silent and disorienting world of grey, of looming rock and vertiginous drops. 'Are we going to be all right getting back down?' asked one of my friends, with a slight tremble in her voice. By her side, a child looked up with a vulnerable, worried face from within the hood of her anorak. I was looking at Wainwright's chapter on Haystacks. Turning to the section on descents, I saw this sentence: 'The best advice I can give to a novice fellwalker lost in mist on Haystacks is to kneel down and pray for deliverance.'

'Oh, we'll be fine,' I said hoarsely, and took out my compass with a shaking hand.

And we were. As fast as it came the mist went, and we clambered down to Buttermere via Scarth Gap glowing with satisfaction. Wainwright had, of course, gone on to offer some rather more practical advice about good lines of descent, and we'd taken it. Down the years since then I've had many an occasion to thank AW (as everyone knows him) for sound advice in tight corners, for illuminating titbits on flora and fauna and fell, for inspiration and consolation. And I've cursed him, too, for his occasional vagueness, his blithe disregard for private land and bad-tempered farmers ('That bloody Wainwright's not very popular round here,' said one churl when I tried to follow AW's route across his pasture) and for his infuriating self-righteousness ('All fellwalking accidents are the result of carelessness,' he once opined, which must be scant consolation if you've just been blown off an arête by a sudden gust). And yet, and yet ...

As William Blake put it, 'Great things are done when men and mountains meet. This is not done by jostling in the street.' The hills bring out the best in people, up there, where things really matter and you can get things in perspective. No one will cut you up or not let you in; if you slow down for someone to overtake you on Striding Edge or let someone come through as they descend Rossett Gill, they will thank you properly, full-bloodedly, not with that haughty raised finger that passes for politeness amongst motorists. They will stop and ask you where you've been, where you're going, pat your dog, offer it a bit of pork pie, offer you a bit of pork pie if you're lucky. If you take a surly early teen with you up a fell, the first thing they will comment on is that everyone speaks to each other. At first they will roll their eyes at this, being at the stage when all human contact that doesn't involve giving a lovebite is 'like, so embarrassing'. But soon they begin to like it, and eventually they become positively hail-fellow-well-met, slapping unsuspecting passers-by on the back and calling them 'mate'.

Start small. Get a few easy ones under your belt. Loughrigg Fell near Grasmere is the perfect short day out and entrée to the joys of Wainwrighting. It begins with a gentle climb on the rough terrace above the lake, enough steepness in the middle to make you feel you're doing something serious and then a summit to die for. Wainwright said that Loughrigg has a bulk out of all proportion to its modest altitude, and *Dalesman* magazine commented, 'It is easy to get lost among the knolls and little tarns of Loughrigg Fell.' Well, possibly, if you're the kind of person who can get lost in the cold meats section of Tesco's. We just stood open-mouthed before the vista of Grasmere and Rydal, the Fairfield Horseshoe, behind us two stretches of Windermere, a bit of Elterwater. And it all looked just like AW had drawn it in his book. This was a revelation. He'd actually been here and actually drawn these hills. Look, that one's Heron Crag and those are the Langdale pikes and that must be Wetherlam. It was so perfect and detailed that I was almost surprised that he hadn't included the fellow having his banana sandwich by the trig point.

Steel Knotts in the beautiful valley of Martindale is not a tough fell, but even it is a kind of a challenge. It's a different challenge, though, than the ones life usually throws at you. Recently some friends and I ended up in some real difficulties on its bracken-clad slopes, muddy, wet, sliding about, risking some of our most valued and tender parts on barbed wire fences at just that height, jumping streams, falling into peat bogs. We arrived back home to a remote lodge with no electricity and erratic hot water tired, bruised, sore, sodden, filthy ... and exhilarated. This was not the nerve-jangling, unsatisfying, febrile stress that comes with deadlines and meetings and presentations and being bullied by the boss, but the proper soul-deep tiredness that comes with physical effort and mental stimulation and maybe just a dash of fear out in fresh air in a beautiful landscape.

These are the days you remember when you're back in the narrow confines of routine. I once read a wonderful passage about opening a guide book, possibly a Wainwright, and the author coming across a blade of grass, one that had found its way there on a walk, and of the feeling of being reminded by this blade of grass: it 'reminded me that I was once a free man on the hills'. Sometimes, on a fetid tube train or in a tedious meeting, we have all felt that we will never be free men and women on the hills. But there's no rush. The hills are not fickle, they are not moody, they are not changeable, they will always be there and at heart they will always be delighted to see you, whether they are frowning through the murk or smiling in the sun.

Last year, a decade or so and several hundred fine, wild, balmy, terrifying, funny, scorching, snowy, blissful, unforgettable days in the hills later, I notched up my 214th and final fell – Kirk Fell, a forbidding hulk in the remote and sombre valley of Wasdale, thus joining a small band of about

500, it's thought. And then champagne and fish and chips for twenty-two in a rented Cumbrian castle. My wife gave me a Wainwright first edition and we toasted the great man, who went to the great chippy in the sky. They scattered his ashes by his favourite spot, the aforementioned lonely, magical Innominate Tarn on Haystacks. Innominate is a beautiful name that actually means 'nameless'. After AW's death a brief, well-meaning but utterly misguided campaign sought to have it renamed Wainwright Tarn. Betty put a stop to that instantly. AW would have hated it, as would anyone with an ear for loveliness, I think.

And Wainwright did have that ear. This is how he ended Book 7, the final volume, the culmination of his labour of love and life's work:

The fleeting hour of life of those who love the hills is quickly spent, but the hills are eternal. Always there will be the lonely ridge, the dancing beck, the silent forest; always there will be the exhilaration of the summits. These are for the seeking, and those who seek and find while there is yet time will be blessed both in mind and body.

Make that time. You won't regret it.

How to Tell the Difference between ...

Swallows, Swifts and House Martins

One of the perennial problems at this time of year is figuring out whether the bird that just flew overhead at the speed of light was a swallow, a swift or a house martin. But fortunately, whilst these birds are all superficially similar, there are a range of differences between them that can make telling these three bird species apart reasonably simple, once you know what to look for.

Swallows

Swallows are most easily identified by their red chin and the longer feathers on either side of the tail, which stick out like streamers and make them easy to spot in flight.

Swifts

Swifts are one of the most amazing birds, barely ever coming to ground to rest except to nest and spending virtually their whole life on the wing. High pitched screeching and curved, sickle-shaped wings, together with a short tail, help to identify this species, which can often be seen on warm summer days performing acrobatics in the sky as they hunt for their insect prey.

House Martins

The house martin is probably the smallest of these three species and has a gently curved tail, unlike the squarer tail of the swift or the 'streamers' of the swallow. They are most easily identified, however, by their white rump, which can often be clearly seen even from some distance as these birds fly past.

Oysteropolis

Michael Smith

T he first inkling of excitement comes on the platform, into the open air, away from the hectic, crowded claustrophobia of the Victorian station and its labyrinthine underground tunnels; there seems to be a note of ozone, a blustery coastal freshness in the air already, cutting through the sticky city heat.

The train gently picks up speed as it glides across the wide sweep of the Thames, the fairy lights on the Albert Bridge a pearl necklace on the grand old dame; past the back of Battersea Power Station, South London, the unfamiliar half, rolls by, 5,000 terraced streets becoming steadily more suburban, gardens and commons getting the upper hand, the city eventually giving way to lush Kentish green, a green so fertile and enchanting that London, as always, has instantly left me, and I am alone in a present-tense romance with the stuff. Kentish countryside seems somehow unlike other English countryside. It's more like the green of

France. It's hard to pin down why. It's like the fairytale French countryside of summer holidays, of childhood and youth.

An hour later the green gives way to luminous blue, and then it's my stop. Stepping back onto familiar ground, walking down the terraced hill to the sea, though the sea here is not quite yet the sea: this seaside is ambiguous, it's almost the shoreline of the Thames still, it's marine and estuarine at the same time. The north bank of Essex is just visible twenty miles away on the far horizon. You are always aware that this is the end of the Thames, and by association the Smoke. Looking inland, you see all the electricity pylons marching off to a smokestacked horizon. The train rumbles past along the same vector of communication and joined-upness, all the way back to the great scabby tit of mother London this Kentish suckling depends upon. It feels like London's last outpost, my bolthole, at this place where the leviathan finally loses out to the vastness of the sea, the vastness of the marine sky, the vasty blue world beyond.

Walking along the shoreline in the pearly evening light, the room above the tennis courts full of stoner kids rehearsing their floydy tunes, wah-wah guitars and jazzy drums floating out of the window which is open to the sea and the balmy summer evening breeze, the best rehearsal room in the world ... past the weatherboarded white pub stuck out on its own on the beach, with old white-haired ponytailed geezers and Floyd proper on the jukebox – there's just something about seaside towns and stoners, I guess ...

An old dear on a fold-out beach chair painting the sea view; all the workaday problems you circle round and round, that blinker you and bind you to your worries and routines, are slowly shed, out here before the wide open sky, the magnificent distance of the far horizon ...

I didn't mind that I'd followed the warm, beckoning smell of frying cod batter down the winding alleys, but missed the best chippy by a whisker; I didn't mind that the other chippy's gear was sloppy and not up to scratch; I didn't even mind that Whitstable had been invaded by swarms of little bugs that got into the hairs on my arms and up my nose every few seconds: here I was, back in my coastal Kentish paradise.

Beyond the ramshackle fishermen's cottages, half a million quid in their battered, black-tarred weatherboard, every Londoner's wank fantasy of a seaside escape, is the real working harbour, where I always end up having a sit and a stare: an ugly corrugated iron silo, sheds, bright yellow diggers piling into huge mounds of sand and gravel waiting to be shipped off somewhere else. It is here, sitting in my own secret quiet spot on the dock, staring at these piles of aggregates, that my soul finally finds its rest, poised between a man's need for bloke stuff and the memories of the child and the moody adolescent who is father to the man; this industrial dock is the essence of my early memories, growing up as I did in a dirty northern port, round the corner from corrugated sheds and piles of aggregates like these, which I would wander round as a teenager, spending long, lonely walks searching for myself, whoever that is ...

The white seagulls sitting on the mounds of gravel have given me back the place I grew up in; though where I grew up is 400 miles away, whipped by the cold winds of the North Sea, it is the same place: the sun sets behind the same bend in the bay, above the same mysterious twinkling pinprick lights; you still yearn to know what life is producing those pinprick lights; the atmosphere of seascape and shoreline haunts you, just the same.

The navy blue sea tractor with the wheels bigger and wider than me reverses, with its bright orange lifeboat on the trailer, the whole ensemble the basic block colours of a lifesize Playmobil toy; its amber light flashes round and round, illuminating specks of spitting rain, and I wander on into the violet hour, alone with my thoughts and the vast sky, the pinpricks of Essex towns twinkling along the far horizon, my thoughts turning to hot chocolate and the candlelit cosiness of the hut.

You are always woken up by the early morning light and the ping of golf balls from the course behind the hut, the retirees rising early and filling up their days with the calmer pleasures ... the first half hour waking up follows a familiar ritual: set a coffee pot up on the stove, hook the doors open, fold out a beach chair and survey the sea and sky. The strange thing about this seascape is it looks equally fascinating in good or bad weather, and all the weather in between. It is often in between, never quite making its mind up, and I can lose whole days watching the changes of the sky and sea, the many mood swings of this temperamental estuary god.

I say good morning to my lesbian neighbours. Half of them are lesbians on my stretch; the seaside is a site for sexual liberty, just as it always was. It was also the site of the first flush of romance between me and the missus – this little bit of coast is part of us and our story, it played the role of midwife in our early romance. She brought me to a similar hut a few doors down on date number three; there were storms all weekend, and you couldn't go outside without getting drenched – we didn't, all weekend, and it was heaven … when I told this story to my granny she chuckled with a cheeky glint in her eye and said, 'Aah, memories! Eh, son?'

When we bought this hut a few months later it was the grand romantic gesture – a second home before we even lived together in a first. I bought my half when I was flush, over-reaching myself as one always does in those circumstances, and now all the cash is spent and I can't pay my rent on the poky boxroom in London any longer, it's still the grand romantic gesture, in another kind of way: I dream of eking out the rest of the long lean summer in this hut, living on Weetabix and digestives, with five quid fish'n'chips as my treat; I daydream of dangling a line off the dock wall at high tide and waiting for a crab, taking him home in my bucket, cooking him on the Campingaz stove, cracking him open and eating him – one of the sea's great bounteous luxuries for nowt; in this way beach-hut life transforms poverty into something glorious; the hut was the glory of my flush, flashy times, and now it's the glory of my poverty.

I have no electricity: the emails remain unread, the mobile phone stays off. Candlelight is fine. The sea is as good a bath as any. I like to imagine I am thick in the heart of this solitude, like Thoreau thick in the heart of his forest, far from the entrapments of modern society, but this of course is not true – I am a ten-minute walk from the Co-op, which shuts at ten, which I can stroll up to for fresh supplies of millionaire shortbread or raspberry pop. I am five minutes from the Old Neptune pub, where I can sup a Guinness watching some gnarly old Kentish blues band. Kate comes at the weekend, and brings kindness and food. But still, amongst these comforts that keep me joined up to the world, the effect is the same: I am alone, with the space to find a kind of peace for myself, which is also where the words come.

I lived a solitary seaside existence marked by poverty once before, when I was young, and lost, and didn't know what to do; this time round is markedly different in one important respect: the wind howls, the walls creak like they might cave in, the candlelight flickers, I write all this down, and I am happy. I thank my lucky stars for this seaside retreat – the lucky stars that line up in the vast, sprawling estuarine sky and stand guard above my tiny weather-beaten hut.

On the Road to Damascus

Bill Drummond

I t is normal for young folk to have infatuations with people of the opposite sex, or maybe with their own sex. These infatuations can be with real flesh-and-blood people they see in their day-to-day life, or with a film or pop star. You know this, we all know this.

But I seem to have missed out on these sorts of infatuations. Not that my sex drive has ever been less than driven, you understand, and I am as boringly heterosexual as you can get, it's just I've never been tormented with infatuations in a boy–girl sort of way. But infatuations are still something that from time to time inflame my urges and desires. In a non-sexual way, you understand, but infatuations all the same. When I was much younger it maybe was a certain species of fish, say the Perch or Brown Trout, or maybe a bird – my infatuation with the Black Cap lasted at least a decade. But I've only ever had one infatuation with a variety of fruit. And this infatuation lasted almost twenty years. It is only comparatively recently that I may have been getting over it. The fruit in question is the Damson. And I can pinpoint the occasion when it began. It was in the early '80s. My then wife and I were spending a night in a rather dark and dreary hotel in Gloucestershire. We were returning to Liverpool from a holiday in the West Country. We had our evening meal in the hotel. I think we were the only people in the dining room. For pudding I chose the special, without even asking what it was. What was placed in front of me was a small glass dish filled with a creamy, purply substance and a teaspoon. Some sort of up-market Fool, I guessed. A custard-based Rhubarb Fool had been a staple in my home as a child. But on the loaded spoon entering my mouth I knew I was tasting a taste I had never experienced before. And there is no way I have the literary skills to describe that taste without sounding totally pretentious. But it is definitely the taste highlight of my life. It is up there with seeing The Clash at Eric's on 5 May 1977 for great life-changing moments. After that first taste, nothing would be the same again for me on the taste front. And I am already sounding pretentious. Up until that evening I had never tasted a Damson before, had no idea what one looked like, or even what family of fruit it belonged to.

A few months later, we moved from Liverpool to the Vale of Aylesbury to start a new life. Part of the new life was to be able to spend much more time wandering about the countryside, as I had in my youth. Come the first early autumn I noticed in the hedgerows amongst the usual

Blackthorns and Hawthorns another odd-looking tree, one hanging heavy with a plum-like fruit. They were somewhat larger than the Sloes on the Blackthorns. However deadly a fruit might look I can never resist the urge to put one in my mouth. And anyway there was no serpent up the branches trying to tempt me, so what could the harm be? Just one bite and I knew it was the same fruit that had been used in the dessert in that dark and dreary hotel. A Damson. And there were thousands of them on this tree. It only took a few minutes for me to fill my haversack to the brim.

These initial ones were stewed. They went well with my morning bowl of porridge. A crumble was baked on the Sunday. Over the following two or three weeks I came across numerous more of these Damson trees, in the hedgerows across the Vale of Aylesbury. And nobody else seemed bothered about harvesting this abundant and free wild fruit. The usual types would be out picking Blackberries, but they would all pass the Damsons by. Did they not know what they were missing, or was my palate markedly different to my fellow ramblers and bramblers? The rest of my family did not particularly share my need for a daily intake of Damsons.

But it wasn't just the taste of the Damson, it was the look of the fruit, its blush of pectin on the dark purple skin; the way they hung together in clumps on the bough, almost like bunches of large black grapes.

Over the coming year I would mark with a cross on my six-inch-to-the-mile Ordnance Survey maps of the Vale, whenever I came across a Damson tree. The dozens soon climbed into scores and it was not long before there was a gross of these trees marked on my maps. Far more fruit than even a legion of Drummonds could get through.

Then as I was out walking early one September morning I came across a whole field of them. The trees had been planted purposefully in rows – an orchard of Damson trees. But half the trees were dead or dying. And on those still living the fruit was being left to rot. Further on in my morning walk I came across more of these orchards, all in the same state of neglect. This led me to believe that at some point in the not too distant past there must have been a thriving demand for this prince amongst the plum family.

This was all back in the 1980s when there was no Google to type the word Damson into and learn all there was to know and much else beside about the fruit that so fired my passions. Around that time, when I was not off coercing Echo & The Bunnymen or locked in a recording studio with Jimmy Cauty, I would be spending my working time in the Aylesbury library writing and researching. It was here that I learnt the name of the Damson comes from the name of the city of Damascus, the ancient and modern capital of Syria. That it is believed it was around this city, over 2,000 years ago, that man started to hybridise various types of plums and wild cherries to arrive at this smallish, dark and packed-with-flavour fruit. The biblical story of Saul, on his way to Damascus to persecute Christians, falling to the ground after being blinded by the light and his epiphany and conversion was one that had held a grip on my imagination over the years. I had often wondered when my own road to Damascus epiphany would happen, if not a full-blown conversion of some sort. And when it did, what changes would it make to me? And would I have to change my name like Saul did to Paul or Cassius to Muhammad?

Sitting in the hushed library, my mind was often in a state of being highly inflamed. This could be in regard to planning the Ocean Rain tour, or concerning strategies that The Justified Ancients of Mu Mu might take, or writing my half of the Bad Wisdom books. But back to Damsons. In the extensive local history shelves of the library I learnt the cultivation of the Damson was once a large-scale local industry, an industry confined to only a few parishes of the Vale of Aylesbury and nowhere else in the British Isles. It had begun to flourish when the Victorian railway builders connected the Vale with other regions of the country. But the industry declined rapidly after the Second World War. Once we could get bananas and oranges and all sorts of other exotic fruits from around the globe, it seemed we lost our palate for the many locally grown seasonal fruit.

Since then the fruit in those orchards had been left to, if not wither on the vine, rot on the branch.

But further reading revealed even stranger reasons for its decline. It seemed this fruit was not only cultivated for its taste but the skins produced a dye highly prized in Luton by the hatters and milliners. You did know that Luton was the hat-making capital of the Empire and the local football team are called the Hatters? If not you should have done, and anyway you know now. But it was not just the milliners of Luton who prized the dye made from Damson skins. Through the 1930s, as Hitler was gearing up the Third Reich, he could not get enough of the Damson skins to dye the uniforms of the Luftwaffe. To think those Heinkels were manned by men wearing uniforms dyed by Damsons grown in the Vale of Aylesbury, as they flew over to drop their not-so-gentle bombs.

No wonder the local farmers gave up on their Damson orchards when the rumours of their very special war effort started to spread. They attempted to spread a counter-rumour, that the uniforms of our very own Royal Air Force were dyed using their patriotic Damsons, but the damage had already been done. Anything connected to the Damsons was connected with supporting the enemy. In fact Damsons were the enemy within.

But as the orchards were left to die another feral population of Damson trees started to spread and take root along the hedgerows that criss-crossed the Vale.

In early '93 I moved into a small and in-need-of-repair farmhouse. From its south-facing windows I had a magnificent view across the Vale. Surrounding the house were five black-barked trees of little account. Useful to string my washing line between, and that was about it. But in those three or four weeks between the pure white of the Blackthorn blossom and the blushed pink of the Hawthorn blossom exploding down the local hedgerows, these five dark trees burst forth with their large and delicate white blossoms. It took the appearance of this blossom for me to recognise these five trees to be Damsons.

It was the appearance of the blossom in my garden which caused my imagination to start tearing in too many directions all at the same time. In my fevered mind it was all beginning to make sense. Because I had never ventured forth on the road to Damascus seeking any sort of epiphany or even full-blown conversion, Damascus had sent out her envoys to track me down and get me. So over the past 1,947 years since Saul fell to the road blinded by the light, those fruit-bearing trees had been heading west. Century by century they were getting closer to me, arriving at the Vale 170 years before me. And even after they were left to die as traitors in their orchards before I was born, they had started their feral march along the hedgerows until they got to this small white farmhouse on a hillside. Five of them forming a guard around the building, waiting for me to come. And once I entered the house, like a lobster into a pot, they would ensure there was no escape for me. Those five wild Damson trees provided me with all the Damsons I could use. There was a large freezer in my workshop, whose only job was to house my year's supply of frozen Damsons. And then there were the shelves of jars containing Damson jam and the demijohns of Damson brandy. And the handwritten book that I kept to collect all the recipes that I could find that used Damsons in some way – it had the flippant title of 'Damsons in Distress'.

But if there has been a conversion, I am still waiting to find out what it is. Life marches on; my solitary life in the house lasted a matter of months. There was soon a woman with a swelling belly, followed by the patter of tiny feet and then some more. But, to quote an old colleague, 'Nothing Last Forever'. Things fall apart and hearts break, and it is some years since I left that house. Driving past it last year, I noticed the new owner had uprooted those five feral and rather useless trees. Maybe their job had already been done. But last autumn I drove out of London, with my youngest son, for a few hours' fishing. We sat holding our rods on the bank of the Aylesbury arm of the Grand Union Canal. The Perch began biting. My son hooked a fine-looking half-pounder. Then while waiting for my float to bob I heard something drop on the ground beside me. Looking down I saw a Damson. I picked it up and popped it in my mouth. The taste was like it was the first time. Looking up, there was a tree heavy with fruit begging to be plucked. Somehow I had not noticed it when we first arrived. I filled my bag and that evening a glorious crumble was made with them. The Damsons have not given up on me yet.

This spring, as the blossoms on all those feral Damson trees across the Vale will be bursting into flower, I will be flying to Damascus, where I will be leading a performance by The 17. The performance will be of Score 328: SURROUND. It will be performed by 100 local members of The 17; each of them positioned 50 metres apart along the

5 kilometres of Damascus' ancient but still standing city walls.

Maybe it is not too late for that conversion.

Postscript: And a rather strange one. I bought the house from an old sailor; he had told me that once he had retired and his wife had to put up with him all the year round, they were finished – she realised they had nothing in common. He also told me how he had bought the house from a comedian he had never heard of, and based on his dealings with this comedian he was one of the least humorous men he had ever met. The name of this not very famous or funny comedian was Peter Cook. It seemed that this Peter Cook's previous marriage had failed due to his heavy drinking and his new young wife was going to save him from his wayward ways by imprisoning him in the small farmhouse on a hill with no ready access to the Soho drinking dens where he had practised his wayward ways. It seems she failed in her attempts. A Peter Cook biography came out while I was living in the house. I was keen to see what mention was made of it in the book. But hardly any was. There was a photo of him in the garden with one of the Damson trees in the background, but it was a mere stripling at the time of the photo being taken. I wonder if Peter Cook ever ate one of the Damsons from those trees, or if he had any sort of conversion on a road to Damascus or anywhere else?

Postscript to the Postscript: I have just read the Peter Cook Wikipedia page to see if it mentioned him living in the farmhouse in question. But there is no mention of it. What I did notice is that he died at the same age as I am now, due to severe liver damage. At least I have not as yet been converted to the bottle. Maybe in time.

How to Catch Trout

Charles Rangeley-Wilson

The short of it:
- find your passion
- learn to feel the flow of a river
- learn to read where the trout are
- learn that a short cast is better than a long one
- learn how drag is everything
- learn that one fly is better than twenty
- learn to go slow and sit still

And the long of it:

Ireland gave me my first trout. I went there every summer in my teens, to stay with a pal of mine – Simon – at his mother's and my godmother's house near Caherdaniel in Co. Kerry. The first year we took the train from Paddington, bikes in the goods van, 'London Calling' on the tape deck. I seem to recall Milford Haven ablaze, an orange firmament dancing on the underside of clouds as we set sail.

Maybe it always looked like that. The ferry smelt of sick and bleach but it was exciting just to be crossing the waters. I didn't sleep much and woke early to watch the green, rolling pastures of the Cork estuary slide slowly by. The seventy-mile bike ride from Cork to the far end of Kerry – past the highest pub in Ireland where chickens roamed the bar – took us a full day and my arse was sore at the end of it. But I was used to cycling then and at the far end we cycled a whole lot more. Rods over handlebars we pounded the Ring of Kerry tarmac from Waterville to Sneem and back again, and though we fished more or less every day, for a long time that first summer we caught absolutely nothing – though our enthusiasm was undimmed. Days rock-hopping Lamb's Head, evenings at the disco in Casey's Cove: all this added up to an idyllic summer in my book, fish or no fish. But I remember the very first finned creature – a flounder – hooked off Derrynane. Simon reeled it in, jumped up and down with joy, lit a cigarette, made a victory sign and hit it on the head. We ate it and it didn't taste of much, other than success, but after that fishing seemed easy.

We got better at our sport and soon pollack and wrasse were caught. Simon was never happier than when he was sitting on a rock, fag in gob, doing his best to look like Terry Hall, waiting for one of those marine beasties to pull his string. Something else pulled me, though, down the road to a stream that drained Eagles Hill, the valley ending in rock and cloud out of which spilled a mercurial, frothy torrent. It fell quickly down the steep hill, past an ancient hill-fort to Castlecove, where, for the last few hundred yards before it hit the sea, the stream slowed enough to allow a bit of weed to grow on the engine blocks that made a riffle under the bridge of the N70. The river turned a long corner around the back of some kind of junk yard or bus depot, and a few of the old lumps of iron no longer needed or able to power western Kerry's wheezy old buses had rolled down that bank into the Castlecove river. In those last few lazy pools, which no one else ever fished and no one ever stopped me from fishing, were enormous brown trout. Some went to 8 oz. I didn't know how to cast a fly then and wouldn't have been able to anyway – the place was a thicket of gorse and overgrown trees that turned the deepest pools into blackened caves of possibility. I had a short, green spinning rod that I'd built in the school hobby-room and a croaky old Invicta fixed-spool reel. I used a worm – no floats or lead – flicked upstream and drifted back towards me. I watched the line for takes. They came thick and fast. The river, like most Irish rivers I have since fished, was full of trout. Sometimes several small fish would grapple with the same outsized lob-worm. And sometimes a whopper would slide out from the drowned roots of the streamside trees or from behind a crank-case, to engulf it whole. I still remember the first. It jumped clear of the water and danced like crazy on the end of the line and was just so damn pretty. I fell in love with trout then and, locked inside 'The Song of Wandering Aengus', I've been fishing for them ever since.

I wonder then if the best way of describing *the how* is to start at the beginning with *the why*: if at the beginning of the how there is a passion – encompassing all the associated meanings of that word: desire, compulsion, infatuation – once found it will guide the rest of the discovery. With passion in your tackle bag the how will ultimately take care of itself. Which is not to say, of course, that it is impossible to light the way, or that there aren't simple directions worth taking.

So why catch a trout? Fishers love to play that one-fish-ever-after game: which fish – you've only got one – would you chase for the rest of your days to the exclusion of all others? I've thought about it often enough now to know there's nothing to think about any more. The answer is the brown trout. The indigenous British and Irish trout, the same fish no matter where you find it, though it can look so different from one river to the next, the Victorians, who were a little incontinent with their taxonomic classifications, named a zillion different species. They're all crammed into one now: *Salmo trutta*. But in appearance the brown trout can vary so vastly you can understand why the stovepipe-hatters got so lyrical.

From Loch Leven brown trout are silver, small-headed with a peppering of black spots, the slightest iridescence of a purple haze along each flank. From the River Itchen they are deep, short, heavy-shouldered, the silver has blended with butter, the black spots have swelled and along each flank, like a series of holes peeping through to a furnace within, is a strafing of the brightest vermilion. From Lough Corrib I've seen trout with sides like coal dropped in sand; from peaty Scottish lochs trout like slabs of dark chocolate. And there's a river I know in Dorset where every fish you catch will have an orange adipose fin – like a candle flame alight underwater. These limitless, painterly riffs around the theme of trout are one reason behind my obsession. They are so bloody pretty, and no two trout look exactly the same: this fact is well known to anglers, who'll recognise fish across the years from the spot patterns on their gill covers. There are ancient brownies in my local stream down the road that I must have caught and photographed two, three times. But in that variety the trout is only responding to its environment, to whether the water is dark or clear, the bed of the stream sandy or rocky. We can see this across these cruder dimensions, though the trout kaleidoscopes well beyond our ability to understand why. In some chimerical way the narrative of the landscape itself is refined and condensed and accreted in trouty hieroglyphics. Limestone, chalk, slate, shale, sandstone, machair, granite, clay: the surface of these islands grades like a thick slab of plywood tilted on a plane, sanded, chopped and buckled and the language of these rocks is printed on the skins of trout. Would that not be reason enough for a lifelong of chasing?

Those Castlecove fish – I sketched many of them before I ate them for breakfast – had butter bellies, green sides, black backs. They looked like the hillside that grew them. I couldn't imagine how fishing could get much better than it was then, crawling through the snags of gorse and over-grown trees, slipping over boulders, pulling those pretty fish from dark pools that ran like Smithwicks bitter, and cycling home at the end of it all with the best half-dozen in a satchel. In many ways it hasn't. More than that, though, fishing for trout with a worm in the Castlecove stream taught me some of the big things I needed to learn about catching trout. Most of all, how to get close to them and where they lay. Two intertwined ideas I would have done best never to forget, though forgotten they were and often are once the angler demands space for his fly-casting and derives too much satisfaction from how well it is going. Trout, I found out then and remember again from time to time, are best caught or tried for under your feet, even with a fly rod. And if you go at it slowly enough that's often where you'll find them.

You can't cast far with a free-running lob-worm. All you have, to pull the line off the reel, is the weight of the worm. And you must cast it with a gentle pendulum swing or it will fall off the hook. You'll struggle to get it more than twelve feet up the river, and an unweighted worm sinks only slowly through the water. If the stream is fast and you hold the worm in the rush of water it will be back past you in seconds, skimming on the surface at the end of a taught line and no trout on earth will take it. So try again, only just to the side of the faster current this time, using the worm and the thin thread that attaches you to it to search for the back eddies and the slips of current between the downstream flow and its upstream counterpart, or the sometimes motionless tongues of water, or the small vortices that will pull the worm down to where the fish are. Only a worm at the mercy of the currents – like a kite in the breeze – can teach you quite so quickly how to feel and read those currents. You must keep the line taut enough that you will see a bite, but not so taut that you're dragging the worm around unnaturally. Soon enough your rod top is tracing every nuance in the flow, you're feeling the river as if you're part of it, and then … tap, tap, tap. A trout is knocking on the door. Where was it? You'll have noticed without noticing. Each time a trout takes, and all the times one doesn't, you'll learn a little bit more about where they lie and where they don't lie. You'll start to read the water, to see the way a river flows across its crests and hollows, weeds and stones, along the corrugated edges, the riffles and undercuts, and you'll start to translate what you see into an idea of where the fish are. The river becomes a language, and that language – admittedly with strange local dialects – is the same for every river: for the moorland stream, for a chalk stream, for a lowland brook in a vale of clay; and once you start to look at them as very big pools on a river, the language is not unfamiliar on a loch or a lough too.

Most universally? The trout are in the seams: not in the rip, nor in the dead water to the side of it. The trout lie between the two. This seam between the tongue of flow into a pool and the dead water to the side of it is the most obvious of all. But think about the margins between fast water and slow across the full three dimensions of the channel: along the bed, along the edges, at the tails of pools, in the whorls off fallen timber or boulders. These seams are the pockets of shelter from which a trout can easily dart into the flow to feed and back again. Think seams, pockets and margins and you won't be far from the fish.

I learnt how to cast a fly eventually and graduated from bicycle to ancient VW Polo and drove over to Kerry every summer for years, camping or hiring caravans near Waterville to haunt the little mountain loughs and streams above Lough Currane. No trees, see? Unlike Castlecove, a bit of space to wield a fly rod. I have pinned to the wall above my desk the Suirbheireacht Ordonais No.20 Dingle Bay bought on one of those hols in Co. Kerry and it's there to remind me of these places: the stream full of engine blocks and one other spot in particular: a necklace of loughs that curls back into the mountains above it – into the foothills of Macgillycuddy's Reeks. We'd park at the end of the road, turn our back on Lough Derriana and follow a little stream up into the valley above. Flat ground at first, a peaty bog crossed by fences hanging with sheep's wool and plastic, then a moraine of mossy, hollow land strewn with boulders, the stream coming and going, above ground, below it, the lough forever over the next brow – until finally we reached it. Tooreenbog was in most lights an almost melancholic body of water. Though it was full of fish, had we not walked beyond it the first time we might never have gone back. But at its head was a waterfall that seemed to invite an exploration of what lay beyond. The valley curled away, its end beyond sight, but with some sort of siren call about the place. We heard it and followed and found over every ridge a new lough, smaller than the last, each one pocked with rising trout and dripping with silence, until we reached the end, a sheer wall of rock 500 feet high, split by a waterfall dropping off the plateau above to vaporise against fern-covered rocks below. The final lough, which doesn't have a name, was pressed up hard against this slope and its windless surface reflected the place like glass. It is a cliché of rose-tinted memory, but here it was true: with a team of three flies I could bet on three to the cast in those loughs, and especially below the waterfall in Tooreenbog.

A good place to practise, then. Because though you can learn to cast a fly rod on a lawn it is much more fun if keen and hungry trout are there to reward your efforts. A lough is good for other reasons: you can find a shore to put the wind at your back; the hungry fish won't mind a muffed cast; the still water gives you time to think. Like everything in fishing, casting a fly rod can get as complicated as you want it to. It can certainly become an end in itself. And above all a brown trout lough will teach you this: like on the stream at Castlecove, if you're quiet and slow you don't have to cast very far. The trout in a small mountain lough are most often feeding right along the edge: if you stand high on a rock and cast at the horizon (which, when you get good at casting, you will definitely spend several years doing) they'll move just beyond reach. If you sneak low and quiet and fish along the shore-line you'll catch a hat-full. So, if we stick with the idea that casting is about catching, it is best kept short and accurate and best kept simple. The casting stroke is this: nine o'clock on the forward stroke, half-twelve on the back. Pull out three yards of line and swish the rod back and forth between these two points. You will have already done it wrong. I said twelve-thirty: that's just past your ear. The rod must never go further back than this! You think it didn't? It did. And again, just now when you tried to prove it didn't. Okay. Do this for an hour, imagining that I am there to tell you ALL THE TIME that you brought the rod too far back. After a while, if you believe me, you might begin to get it right. You'll know when you have because the line will straighten along the ground in front of you, instead of falling in a heap. By the way, you'll be taking it too far back for two reasons: first, you are flopping the wrist; second, you'll be waving your elbow around. Tuck the elbow in at the hip. Don't break the wrist.

When you've finally got that right try the same again with a longer line: it'll probably go wrong again. You'll compensate for the added length by making those same mistakes you started with and you'll add to the mix the idea that if you swish really quickly it will help. In fact you need to slow down. Stop the rod at twelve-thirty, remember the wrist, remember the elbow, and now give the line a fraction of a second longer to straighten out behind before you bring it forward again. Good.

It probably goes okay sometimes and not so okay others. And the weird thing you'll have noticed is that the harder you try the worse it goes. There doesn't seem any natural way out of this. Of course I need to TRY HARD TO GET ALL THIS BLOODY LINE OUT THERE. Thing is, with fly casting, you're not really doing the work: the rod is. Trying harder, swishing it faster, grunting, getting in a fizz … it's all a bit like flapping your arms to get the plane to take off.

Casting a fly rod is all about timing, not strength or effort, and the harder you try the more you'll lose the timing. Slow down. Chillax. The rod is a spring and you load it with the inertia of the fly line; it moves forward and stops and uncoils its energy down the line; you pull back and load it again, and so forth. Unless you're loading and unloading the rod you're not doing anything. So the best image I can leave you with is this: imagine you've got a brick on roller skates, attached to a thin string. You have to move the brick forwards and backwards. If you yank the string it will break, or maybe the brick will fall off the skates. If you go gently and get the timing right it will work just fine.

Anyway, that was all on the toughened west coast: small brownies, four to the pound and hungry as hell. When I got a job teaching Art to school kids I moved to Dorset and fell inside chalk-stream country. Now the fishing was really tricky. Chalk streams rise from underground, feeding cool, clear and constant flows to lush valleys in which everything grows – fat trout and the fat flies them make them so – to an abundance. Chalk streams are the origin of dry-fly purism, the idea that educated trout develop OCD not only about which fly they'll eat, but also about exactly which stage of the insects' eclosion they will fixate on. And sometimes it really does work like this. It can be a fun puzzle to unlock when it does. Most of the time, though, these pampered trout are as catholic in their diet as any other. The fish you thought was taking only blue-winged olives will have beetles, caterpillars and gnats in its belly. What chalk-stream trout do have, though, is an enhanced sense of caution. All trout are cautious, constantly offsetting the need to eat against the desire not to get eaten. But the more there is to eat the higher trout set the barrier against being fooled, the keener their already acute awareness of what looks natural and what doesn't. In fly fishing that known acuity on the part of the fish translates most often into this: an angler's obsession with fly pattern. Wrongly. The wrong fly presented naturally will get eaten way, way, way more often than the right fly presented unnaturally. And natural presentation of the fly is all about understanding the currents.

Back to Castlecove. The worm on the end of a short line has taught you to feel the river.

But now the fly on the end of a longer line will feel, at first, like playing a guitar in gloves. Though we can impart some control to it, the fly line won't move like the top of your rod did when you were learning how to fish with the worm. Once cast it lies more or less inert on the water, prey to whatever the flows are doing along its length. And that is unlikely to be the same as what the water is doing around the fly. The river might be moving slowly under the fly line, but quickly under the fly. Or the other way about. You've already felt how the river is a marbled conflict of currents. This conflict between the way the water pulls at the fly line and the fly is called drag: the way the fly is pulled, sometimes to an infinitesimal degree, so that it moves unnaturally on, or within, the water.

Drag is everything in fly fishing. Drag is what stops most fish from taking your fly.

Though I started to understand this in Castlecove, it's taken me thirty years to truly get it. Every season scales fall from my eyes and I remember all over again. If you're casting at a fish that just will not take the damn fly, though it keeps on rising and the pattern looks about right (I'll get to what that means later), eight times out of ten it's drag that is screwing you up. Even if you can't see it … that's what it is.

It would be impossible to summarise how you deal with drag. It is in itself as infinitely various as the river that imparts it. Drag is one of the beauties of fly fishing. It isn't an enemy, so much as one of the things that makes the whole business so compelling. Don't resent it, but do be aware of it and know that no matter what other bullshit you'll be told about flies needing red eyes, and blue testicles, grey wings and eight tails, or what you'll feel compelled to believe about how a new fly-rod or line or reel will unlock the door to better fishing, it's all nonsense in the face of drag. A chasing after the wind. Master drag, my son (or at least start to understand it) and you will truly be an angler. Fish a dragless fly off the end of a garden cane and you'll catch more trout than King Croesus and all the techno garb that his gold would have bought him.

Impossible to summarise but for one rule: the closer you get to the fish the less drag will affect your fly line. Wade quietly and slowly – and I mean *quietly* and *slowly* – and you'll be amazed how close you can get to a feeding trout. The biggest city trout I ever caught I cast at for over an hour. He (it was a he, all right) was hidden in a dark part of the stream where it flowed between a chain-link fence and a paint-shop, under a tunnel of overgrown branches and ivy. I couldn't so much cast under there as flick, and so achingly slowly I inched forward until I was on my knees in the mud alongside him and could reach out the rod and drop a fly onto the stream over his head, retrieve it in a low sweep and start again. Twice the fish had to move out of the way of rolling beer cans, and once I swear it took a sweet wrapper for a mayfly. I must have cast at that trout over 100 times with better patterns than a sweet wrapper. And what separated that final cast, the one when the fish took the fly, from all the others, that made the fly float like the sweet wrapper? Only drag. Or lack of it.

Which is not to say that the fly you use doesn't matter, only which comes first.

It was the summer of '95 – when the chalk streams I fished in Dorset were drying up – that I went back over the sea and discovered the limestone streams of inner Ireland.

Richard had found us this cottage to rent, stuck perfectly between his salmon on the Blackwater and my trout on a stream called the Awbeg. The Awbeg flowed through lightly grazed meadows, full of wild orchids. Snipe drummed overhead. It flowed fast and clear over clean gravel and beds of ranunculus. In the deeper parts it curled like a cat's tail past stands of flag iris. It was the Platonic ideal of a trout stream. Below the village of Castletownroche, in the final couple of miles before it met the Blackwater, it fell into a deep wood. There, standing ruined in the trees, was an old mill, and below it a pool that I lost hours on. Insects hatched there in such profusion that as the evening wore on, though trout would rise continuously, if I wanted to keep catching them I *had* to change patterns to keep up with whichever fly they had turned their attention to – hatching olive or ovulating sedge or sherry spinner. This is when fly pattern really matters. I suspect it doesn't matter as much as it used to. It is profusion that causes it and this little river somehow had escaped the pesticides and abstraction and road run-off that have done for profusion elsewhere. Taken to an extreme, though, preparation for events like this would blow your mind. Most of the time, then, it's best kept either simple or extremely simple. The latter is where to start. Flies are expensive enough before you tie your own. Extremely simple then: if you asked me to fish with one fly for a whole season but allowed me to have it in every size, I could catch nearly as many (or few) fish as I ever do with a *Klinkhammer* tied in grey and brown. If you gave me one more, but again allowed all sizes, I could mop up most of the remainder with a *gold-head hare's ear nymph*. Throw in the luxury of a third and a *sparkle caddis* in all sizes would be my choice. Graduating to simple I might add: *daddy-long-legs* for the autumn, *hawthorn* flies for the spring, *ants* and *sherry spinners* for the summer. A selection of *buzzers* (midges) for the lakes. Maybe a small *fry* pattern. You'll go way, way beyond that lot and back again by the time you've finished. There will be others who swear by an *Adams*, or an *F-Fly*. None of us are wrong. It all boils down to this: most of the time colour doesn't matter at all. Tone might matter, but not much. Shape matters a lot. Size matters most of all. Sadly pattern probably mattered a lot more 100 years ago, when rivers were cleaner and had denser, more complicated hatches of flies, the sort of hatches that induce obsessive, pernickety appetites in trout. If you bump into a hatch like this, sure you'll do better with the right fly, but if you go slowly and quietly, get close, cast accurately and master drag, you won't do badly with the wrong one.

Which brings us round, in an appropriately meandering way, to the *satori*, the *wu* of angling for trout. Zen master Isaak Walton nailed it when he wrote 'study to be quiet', and he was only quoting Thessalonians. This *satori* in fishing is the ability to sit still and watch the river, to wait for it to speak to you. A good angler goes slowly, treads lightly. The only time I ever want to be a smoker is when I'm fishing. Smokers have learnt through all the ciggy breaks as they watch the river flow by what the rest of us either miss altogether or only ever notice during lunch – that if you sit still for a while a great big fish will start rising under your nose. A couple of years ago I was fishing with a good friend of mine who is for ever rolling himself medicinal cigarettes. I had brought him to a particular pool where I knew there was a particular fish: a giant of a trout which lived under the barbed-wire fence where it sagged across the water. A fish I had hooked but which had broken my line – and rod – the previous year. Business, as they say, was unfinished. We sat on the bank while Maui rolled himself a big one. But my fish wasn't showing. So Maui lit up and we sat a while longer. It was pleasant enough tucked out of the breeze, soaking up whatever existed of the weak sun. Still my fish stayed hidden. Not a sign. Nothing but the gentle whisper of wind, the lapping of the water, Maui's inhalations. But then this other sound: again and again. Not quite in an even rhythm like a drip, though it sounded like a drip. Like a fat drip hitting a puddle. I started to look around. And then I saw it. Not up there under the fence but right alongside us, in the furrowed ripple the wind was chasing up the channel: the nose of a very big trout making very tiny slurps on the water. We caught it eventually: a five-pound cock-fish. We were right alongside it, the cast was short, there was no drag and the fly was about the right size. But we'd never have even seen it without Maui's herbal dalliance, without 'studying to be quiet'.

Name that Tune

Cheryl Tipp

To be able to identify a bird by its voice alone can be extremely rewarding. The human ear is a highly sensitive device and together with the brain is more than capable of learning and identifying a whole host of bird songs and calls. It just takes practice, patience and a desire to learn. Here in the British Isles we are incredibly lucky to have such a wealth of different birds that enhance our acoustic environment with a huge variety of sounds. In many cases you're more likely to hear a bird rather than see it, especially in habitats with plenty of hiding places such as woodlands and reedbeds.

Some birds like to give us a helping hand (or should that be wing?) and actually say their name when they vocalise. The two syllable 'cuc-koo' lets everyone know that a male Cuckoo is in the area, having returned to the British countryside from his African wintering grounds. This familiar harbinger of spring is not an easy bird to see, so being able to recognise its distinctive call does have its advantages. Another summer migrant with an onomatopoeic name is the Chiffchaff. This small brown warbler sings a simple 'chiff-chaff' phrase over and over again from the relative safety of trees and shrubs. Again, this is not an easy bird to spot, but the sound of its distinctive song soon gives the game away. The colloquial name for the Lapwing, the Peewit, is derived from its wheezy, drawn-out 'pee-wit' call, while the Curlew takes its common name from the evocative 'cour-loo' cry that can be heard across moors and marshes throughout the year.

Other birds seem to be saying specific sentences, or at least somebody once thought they were and, luckily for us, the phrases have stuck. The Collared Dove produces a loud cooing song that can either be interpreted as 'u-nit-ed' (easy to remember if you happen to be a Man U fan) or 'I don't know'. Just have a listen to the song and hopefully you'll see what I mean. The song of the Yellowhammer takes a little more imagination, but the phrase 'a little bit of bread and no cheese' is a pretty good description of this high-pitched tune that is best heard in and around farmland areas.

In some cases it takes a little more work to learn the different songs and calls, especially when species sound very similar, but there are always little tricks and useful hints to help you on your way. The Blackbird and Song Thrush are closely related members of the Thrush family (Turdidae) and possess songs that on first listening could be confused. The Song Thrush really likes to repeat himself and that trait is the key to successfully identifying this species. Each song phrase is repeated two or three times before the singer moves on to another combination of notes. The Blackbird, on the other hand, prefers to keep things fresh, and even though certain phrases will be repeated the song is less structured and more free-flowing in style. The Skylark has an extremely complex song and it would be hard to pinpoint a particular phrase or pattern of notes that could be used as an acoustic fingerprint. Other measures are therefore required in order to identify this species. The most distinctive thing to note is that the Skylark can literally sing for minutes without taking a break. A breathtaking stream of beautiful warbles and trills pours from this little bird's beak as he soars higher and higher into the sky. The poet Percy Bysshe Shelley described the Skylark's song as 'a rain of melody' in his poem 'To a Skylark', and anyone who has stood beneath an ascending Skylark in full song will immediately appreciate this fitting description.

Some birds try to throw us off the scent by mimicking other species. To be fair these individuals aren't trying to deceive us on purpose. In fact they probably couldn't care less about our efforts to recognise their songs. This is because they are completely wrapped up in the rituals of the breeding season. A great way for male birds to maximise their luck with the ladies is to develop an impressive song. However, being able to successfully mimic and then incorporate excerpts of vocalisations from other species into their song can really help a male stand out from the crowd. The

Blackbird, for example, has a beautiful repertoire at the best of times but being able to add something different or unique to his song can really get the girls swooning. Documented examples of Blackbird mimicry include copying the vocalisations of other birds, the calls of other animal groups, and even the sounds of mechanical devices such as car alarms and computer modems. The Starling is also a fantastic mimic and you could easily be forgiven for thinking you were listening to a barking dog or a crowing cockerel when in fact it was actually a male Starling flexing his vocal muscles.

Of course you don't have to be in the countryside to encounter wildlife. Urban environments offer food and shelter to many species and in some cases you are more likely to come upon certain birds in towns and cities than anywhere else. It's not always easy to single out wildlife sounds when the acoustic environment is saturated with traffic, sirens, building work and the general day-to-day hum of urban life, but with enough practice and attention to detail you can train your ears to filter out the unwanted noise and focus in on those songs and calls. For several consecutive years a male Black Redstart used the wind vane on top of London's St Pancras Station as a song post. Anyone who has passed through this part of the capital will know that it's not exactly the quietest of places. Despite the constant stream of taxis, buses, cars and people, the song of the Black Redstart could still be heard above the madness of rush hour. Granted, the song was somewhat smothered by the general din, but the hurried warble and scratchy jumble of notes was still an audible component of the urban soundscape.

A great way to try out your listening prowess is with a little springtime test. The dawn chorus is one of the highlights of the year for nature lovers and can be experienced in both urban and rural settings. The test will involve getting up early (sorry about that) but I can promise you that it will be well worth it. Immersing yourself in the dawn chorus can be a magical experience. The air is filled with chirps, tweets, sweet melodies and vibrant songs, all of which create a natural symphony that never fails to impress. To begin with, just soak up the atmosphere and enjoy the simple pleasure of listening. Then try to pick out individual songs and calls. The dawn chorus can last for several hours so you'll have more than enough time to do both. Even if you don't necessarily know which species is producing what sound, you should start to identify patterns and rhythms within the general chorus that are being created by different species. Team this awareness with an audio identification guide and you'll soon be able to put names to voices. There's a whole new acoustic world out there just waiting to be explored, so prick up your ears and start listening!

Drinking the
Seasons

Mark Dredge

As the sky passes from grey to blue and the fields roll from brown and bare to golden and glowing, so the beers on the bar flow with them. Bright and fresh for the new life of spring, light and fruity for the summer sun, turning earthier and brown as the sun's glare fades through autumn and into dark and hearty for the bracing winters, beer is as seasonal as the food we eat, wonderfully evocative of the world around it.

Local and fresh is how beer is best, and the ale brews of Britain make use of the ingredients grown nearby, with world-famous crops of barley and hops. As Slow Food gains momentum and as provenance becomes important to many, so that pint before you tells a story of the countryside around you.

For 9,000 years we've been intoxicated by the lure of fermented grain. As cultures grew, passed through generations and travelled, beer developed, and its life story is as long and interesting as the history of mankind itself. As a product of the earth it's simple to make: hops, barley and water make up the base of your pint and the timely addition of yeast gives the salutary alcohol kick; simmer malted grains in water, drain off the resulting sweet liquid, boil it and add something bitter like hops, then add yeast, wait a few days for the yeast to turn residual sugar into alcohol and you've got something resembling beer.

Hops are the bittering agent of choice in modern beers, but this wasn't always so. Herbs, spices and plants would all have been used to counter the sweetness of the malted grains and to give it a more thirst-quenching quality – without the bitterness it isn't something you can drink all day (which is a very important quality when beer is your 'liquid bread' or it's safer to drink than the water). Bittering herbs would've included bog myrtle, yarrow, sage, burdock root, mugwort, orris root, wormwood, rosemary, dandelions, heather, ground ivy, juniper, bay, balm, as well as various spices. New versions of these beers are now brewed, harking back to beers past and giving a suggestion to modern drinkers – a photo for the tastebuds – but now it's the hop that rules.

The history of hops goes back over 1,000 years but it wasn't until the 15th century that they reached Britain, arriving from Northern Europe and rooting in the South of England. Far from being welcomed, hops were hated by many brewers who were yet to be lured by the lupulin charms of the green flowers. Gradually they became the plant of choice, likely, in part, due to their preservative qualities which saw hopped beers lasting longer than those beers made with herbs, which would have soured quickly.

As well as a preservative effect, the introduction of hops into beer imparts bitterness, flavour and aroma, depending on when they enter the brewing kettle – the earlier they are used the more they will add bitterness, while the later additions will boost aroma. Hops are varietal, being products of their parentage and where they are grown, and world regions are renowned for certain styles of hops in the same way that grapes are prized for their position on the world wine map. Historically there wasn't the luxury of choosing to brew with hops from around the world so steadfast styles developed their unique flavours around the ingredients available, meaning that local hops make the local beer styles what they are, and they are still famous for it now.

Saaz, a classic lager hop, is from Žatec in the Czech Republic and gives a light fruity flavour and a dry bitterness, while Hallertau is a German lager hop known for adding a herbal bite – it's also eponymous as one of the premier growing regions of the world; the English Fuggle is a star of the Best Bitter, giving a pungent and punchy earthy bitterness; East Kent Goldings give a floral, spicy poke to English pale ales and bitters; and Cascades of Yakima Valley in Washington State, another major growing area, give a burst of grapefruit in a glass, unmistakable in its fruit and high bitterness with a bold flavour to go in progressive American styles of beer.

Passing through Kent, where they would have settled from Europe 500 years ago, the mark of the hop is easy to see with the red brick turrets and snow-white peaks of oast houses. Most of them are now converted into part of a country house, but their original use was to dry hops ready to be used in brewing. Hops start to spoil soon after they are picked, so they need to start drying as quickly as possible and these oasts plot out a map across the county of where hop fields would once have been.

While there may now be fewer than there once were, the vibrant green hop bines of Kent fill the hot August air with a sticky spiciness just before their September harvest. Unlike the packaged tours to summer sun which we now know as holidays, a century ago, and up until the 1960s, trips to Kent to pick hops were a popular vacation of the working class coming from London and the South East. The holidaying hop pickers combined with itinerant workers and travellers to see 250,000 extra people pass into Kent's countryside each harvest, where they would work from 6 a.m. until late afternoon to strip the bines. Back-breaking and finger-staining, a month in the fresh country air was a good break from London life, taking the children to pick in the morning and allowing them to play in the fields in the afternoon – workers were paid by the basket, so the more hands to help, the more hops in the sack and more money in the pocket: child labour at one of its finer moments.

It's no longer the holiday of choice, with the work going out to hourly-paid labourers, but the harvest is still a celebrated time of year on the brewing calendar. The other late-summer harvest is of the spring barley; planted, as the name suggests, earlier in the year, they reach their golden ascent in August and September when they are ready to be cropped, meaning the important base ingredients of beer are harvested at the same time of year.

When beer is brewed, it's the grain which is the main influencer of style and colour. The major grain for beer is barley, but wheat, oats and rye are also used. Few make the link between waving fields of top-heavy barley to that pint of beer on the bar, which is a shame because these fields are a sight which dominates summer drives and rambles through the country, a dancing crop stretching with the roll of the land, one which movies have made it irresistible not to want to run through with a childlike leap.

Britain is a major grain grower for brewing, with crops prized around the world. Barley is grown across England and parts of Scotland, with major areas including East Anglia, Lincolnshire, Yorkshire and Kent. In order to make it fermentable, the sweet centre of the grain has to be released by a process of steeping in water, drying it so that it germinates and then kilning, turning it into malt. Kilning adds colour and flavour; like toasting bread, when kilning the malt goes from light and sweet, to toasty and caramelised, into roasty and dark and on to black and charred. By adding these in different volumes the brewer creates the base and body of the beer.

With the high sun and heady aromas of the late summer, the countryside of Britain is ready to start the transition from ground to glass, passing the harvests and the preparation of ingredients into the brewhouse, where one thing rules: water. The majority of a pint is made from water, and different chemical compositions of it give different final qualities to the beer – soft water and hard water react differently with the ingredients of beer and produce different reactions and flavours. As beer was, and still is, brewed with water from local sources, this has seen great brewing towns built and grow around the best water sources.

London was once the brewing centre of the world and home to three of the most famous beer styles: pale ale, porter and stout. With pints of porter and stout as dark as a Dickensian villain, London water is ideal for these beers due to the high levels of bicarbonate, which has a neutralising effect on the harsher flavours of dark malt, while the high sodium and calcium content leaves a rounded, smooth flavour. Dublin, the spiritual home of stout thanks to Arthur Guinness, also has water which is high in bicarbonate, making it an ideal location to make the world's most iconic pint. Pilsen, in the Czech Republic, is the home of pilsner, the style which has been copied by the mega breweries around the world. Famously soft, the mineral-free waters of Pilsen add a rounded body to the beer, leaving a very smooth mouth feel and a flavour which enhances the hop profile without overpowering the delicate malt.

But it's Burton-on-Trent which has the most renowned brewing waters, where the hard mineral-rich liquid is high in calcium, magnesium and sulphates which accentuate hop bitterness and leave a dry finish to a beer. It's no surprise that the pale ales of London travelled north to Burton-on-Trent, where their growth found fame locally and as far away as India, to where India Pale Ale (IPA) was exported.

Burton-on-Trent is so highly regarded that the process of 'Burtonisation' refers to the addition of salts and minerals to create the same hard-water profile as Burton (if you ever smell sulphur – boiled eggs – in your beer then it's because of the water, as Burton has a high sulphur content), although the name has developed to mean any treatment made on the water before brewing, giving the brewer the ability to replicate any water in the world and therefore get consistency with the brew or adapt water to best suit a particular style.

At one time, pre-industrialisation, pre-Pasteur and his discovery of yeast, and pre-hops, all beer would have been 'seasonal' and uniquely local, made by the ingredients found nearby – hops or herbs, grain grown in the surrounding fields, water from the nearest source. They would have been drunk locally too (Budweiser was one of the first breweries with a desire for the national and international travel of their beer, dating to the late 19th century). Now consumers are turning back towards understanding the importance of the seasons and provenance and brewing is beginning to follow foodie trends.

Each season, and the weather it brings, has tastes and beer styles to suit the mood and temperament in a lovely symbiotic link between what it's like outside and what we want to drink: the life-is-good-again of spring, the vibrancy of colour, flavour, freshness; the let's-live-life attitude of summer, with long uncomplicated days spent with friends in the sun; the buckling in of autumn, gradually warming ourselves in preparation for the upcoming cold months; and the restorative search of winter, a need for a spike of boozy warmth and a deep comfort within. These yearly-evolving brews fold in and out of the seasons effortlessly, alive with tastes which reflect the changing weather and world around us, suiting the temperament of the moment in a life–beer embrace. The beers also manage to evoke something outside the glass inside it, with unique reflections of flavour.

Coming from the dreary darkness of winter, spring arrives suddenly one day with a gust of fresh air and a surprise sighting of life re-emerging all around; everything is bright and green again, to the great relief of many. With beer, spring is all about one thing: hops. Light-coloured beers are poured with the faintest tinge of green to the edges, as fresh as the daisies peeking out at the sun, and there's a renewed vibrancy to them, a flourish of floral hops, a grassy dryness and a burst of citrus, while still containing a background sweet-ness from the malt to protect from the nippy breeze.

These spring beers are designed to quench a thirst and excite with their full flavours, to promote the hop to the foreground (it played a supporting role to the dark winter beers) while giving a reflected taste of the outdoors: elder-flower or honeysuckle, freshly mown grass, blossom, a bouquet of oranges and tropical fruit, maybe some pine or lime; the flavours of a summer that's coming soon but alive with the harvest just passed. Spring is a season as teasing and hopeful as the sun looking out from behind parting clouds; it says we're alive again and that good things are coming.

Summer is for relaxing with friends, enjoying the sun, barbeques, beaches and beer gardens. We don't want beers which are heavy and complex; we want something that we can drink a few of while socialising and without falling over. With the burst of hops in spring, the summer brews get brighter and lighter as we see golden and pale ales proliferate. Designed for gulping and quenching the thirst, they are fruity and floral with a bite of bitterness at the end to have you going back for more.

Far from having a long-standing tradition of these easy drinkers in the summer, golden ales with a specific warm-weather-extinguishing purpose only emerged in the mid-1980s, thanks in part to a desire to bridge the gap between the ubiquitous cold lagers of continental Europe and the brown bitters of Britain. The original was Exmoor Gold, 'the colour of Chardonnay' and designed to visually appeal to ale and lager drinkers; it's fruity, floral and light, brewed with classic English hops and malt and has inspired many other beers since.

The joy of the summer pint is in drinking it outside. It's the finishing-line promise of a cool beer after the kind of walk which makes your brow damp and your throat dry; it's the beer garden which folds into the local surroundings with its sights and sounds (fields of barley, stretching views of the country, nature playing in your peripheral vision); it's the bottle in one hand and burnt burger in the other, fired black from the barbeque. To think of summer is to think of friends and being outside, and nothing works quite like a pale beer, served cold.

If the arrival of spring comes as a nice surprise, then the fall into autumn is met with sighs of another summer inevitably lost or wasted, to be followed by the down slope into winter. This is probably why autumn is the wild season, starting with the hard work of the harvest, getting scary at Halloween, and exploding on Fireworks Night things seem to get a bit crazy here. For beer it's one of the most exciting and varied seasons, naturally reflecting the darkening days with amber and brown beers, but also heady with spices and earthy depths like the foods of the autumn months.

The harvest is the important moment. Worldwide the bines of hops are stripped while the final spring barley crops are cut for their next destination: the ingredients of the next year are prepared. One of the unique styles of autumn is green hopped beers, using the hops immediately after they are picked. Speed is essential when picking hops so that they can begin the drying process as quickly as possible without spoiling, but brewers can also use them 'wet' from the harvest before drying. These are a snapshot of freshness, a taste of beer in a different state to the usual, comparable to using fresh herbs rather than dried herbs, although there are essential unknowns with fresh hops (they are high in water content so brewers need to use lots more of them than usual; they also haven't been tested for their acid content, which provides bitterness and aroma, something brewers use to calculate projected qualities in the brew); it's a brewing roulette with potentially very exciting results. The best of these beers use the most local hops, sped from the country-side to the brewing kettle in the quickest possible time; a taste of a very specific place and moment.

Then comes the smoke of bonfires and fireworks, with nights spent outside in the cold staring at fires and colourful explosions. The dark beers of autumn come with their earthy bitterness and hints of smoke, often fruity, sometimes spiked with spices. If you could personify an autumn pint it would grow into a firework display – dark but still fruity and lively and capable of bursting with exciting flavours.

Winter is the time for wrapping up warm, ending one year and looking forward to the next. It's here that the beers, like the mornings and nights, reach their darkest. Designed to warm and nourish, they are best enjoyed by a flickering fire where the charry, roasted flavours of the beer match the glow at the toes. Stouts, porters, dark ales, strong ales and barley wines all star in the winter when a cold pint of some-thing pale doesn't quite have the appeal of something hearty and rich. Reminiscent of chocolate, smoke, earth or dried fruits, these beers mirror the tastes and smells all around: roast meats and stews, fruit cake, chimneys, the cold snap of fresh air, dark berry fruits. Just like the other seasons, they reflect a moment, a feeling, a taste within the glass. Not many other products can do this so well.

The other winter seasonal is the novelty Christmas beer. Identified by anything with a pun on Santa, snowballs or

Rudolph, and a design of gaudy reds and greens, these are the ale equivalent of a Christmas jumper. A bit of fun, and some are worthy of attention, but most should be avoided like the drunk at the party with the mistletoe cap.

All of these beers also work effortlessly with the foods available at the time. The punchy spices of spring, with a desire to liven things up with a little heat, work wonders with the tongue-tapping hops. The salads and barbeques of summer love the golden ales. Pumpkins, roast meats and fragrant spices are ideal with the amber and brown beers of autumn. And the gut-filling stews of winter only belong next to a glass of dark, rich beer.

Seasonal beers are a chance for a brewery to try something new. It's an opportunity to flex the brewing muscle on something different, something reflective of the coming season or events, or just something which uses different ingredients: green hop beers, zingy spring liveners with more hops than a rabbit farm, summer refreshers, Halloween frighteners, bonfire brews and Santa's Sack. Many beers are brewed year-round, which means you can find hearty stouts in July and cooling lagers in November, with something to satisfy every thirst; the fun is the choice we have at the bar or in the bottle shop and how we can change tastes through the year when one particular type really comes into its own. There really is a beer for every day of the year.

The joy of seasonal beer is that in some wonderful way it tastes like the world outside: the spring pints are freshly 'green' in a way almost impossible to describe without using words like cut grass and blossom; summer beers are cool and unchallenging, just like the way we want to feel – vibrant, alive, refreshed; the darkening beers of autumn bring smoke and spices, they turn earthier, they evoke harvests and fireworks; intensify this into winter, make them darker and richer and they are hot water bottles, deeply flavoured with roasted malt, chocolate, dried fruit and with a full body like a cuddle for your tongue.

The fold of beers from outside the glass to the inside keeps the bar as interesting as the sights, smells and tastes surrounding it. A product of harvests of the nearby countryside, of ingredients grown there for hundreds of years with the same purpose, it's a special drink with so much history and so much future. And there's nothing nicer than sitting outside and drinking a cool pint taking in the surroundings, or sitting inside and looking outside at the cold day, grateful to be warm. That's when beer and the countryside come together, when we understand how closely they are aligned and appreciate them at the same time.

Reclaiming the Language

Paul Evans

The Swan Riddle

This is a thousand-year-old riddle:

Silence is what I wear when I walk the earth or make my home or stir the waters. Sometimes my beauty and these high air currents take me above the houses and the power of clouds lifts me over nations. My charms resonate strongly with melody, singing when I am away from the flood or the earth – a travelling spirit.

(Adapted from R.K. Gordon, *Anglo-Saxon Poetry*, Everyman, 1964)

Who am I? *A swan.*

Silence, water, flight, beauty, music, travel – long before the Norman Conquest, an English writer posed this riddle about the swan. So this is a translation from Old English into Modern English and the swan, moved by the power of clouds and its own magic, is lifted through a thousand years of the same language.

People we call the Anglo-Saxons brought this language from the river valleys, fens and estuaries of Northern Europe. They came to Britain with swan symbols on their sword handles and swan maidens dancing through their mythology. Our language and swans were both adapted to the same watery landscapes.

We can feel the truth of this on cold winter mornings, when the sun arcs low above lead-grey pools and glints on the white plumage of swans as they slide out of the mist. Silently gliding or splashing wildly, our language struggles to keep up with swans, words like webbed feet slapping the gloss off the water and swooshing with their wings through the air.

And the riddle? A question to confuse and then reveal like a conjurer's trick: the swan flying into the heart of our fluid culture, linking our lakes and rivers to the ancestral north across the sea – which the author of *Beowulf*, the first great poem in English, called 'the Swan's Road'.

Lost Places

I.

I wrote this after kicking snow off my boots against a wall on which hung a thermometer reading −13°C. It was cold all right and I was fortunate not to be stuck in a motorway traffic jam or ghost train or airport from hell. I was free to wander, for my moustache to freeze, for my footprints to colonise a new world. The fog had risen overnight, drawing Arctic breath from fresh snow and blowing it in frost needles over trees and fences. Everything the fog touched had been transformed. Where the hell was I? It was not that I'd lost my way but my way had lost me. I walked from the road through a gate, up a snowy field which was, until recently, pasture with remains of an ancient lane running down it. Visibility was down to just a few yards, and I was following an archaeological route, imagining it as a kind of Braille to be read by walking on earth rather than by placing fingertips on paper.

I reached a stile beyond which the ghost road had long been ploughed up and hedged with a mean little track to corral the walker along a fence. Instead of being shoved that way, I opened a gate into the fog. It was a double aluminium gate, big enough for a machine the size of a house to drive through, and with a fastener like a rat-trap fitted across the top. I took care not to make a sound, even though there was no one around – not that I could have seen them if there were.

I kept close to a hedge where blackthorn twigs, rose-hips and maybe time too were covered with a thick glaze of ice in a bitter wind which poked into a corner where a fallen limestone wall hinted at the remains of a dwelling. There was an enigmatic circle of gaunt old ash trees around a shallow depression. They all seemed to face inwards as if watching something down a hole. I'd lost the gap to another path, so I continued my trespass along hedgerows. Where the hell was I? Suddenly, in the fog above were rooks and robins in the dark tracery of a lime tree, with deep blue sky high above but around it only grey mist and a place once somewhere, now lost.

II.

There were a few drops of blood in the snow, bright as rose-hips and holly berries. From the hoof-skid further up the tracks, the blood had come from a fallow deer. Maybe it was chased by a dog, maybe it was snagged on thorns and maybe it was wounded by one of the shooters banging away in a nearby wood, but the deer ran this way then doubled back in sudden violence. I wondered if blood in the snow tasted of the wind's cold metal.

A white December morning, beyond the breath-steam, may have been beautiful but it was not peaceful. Snow brought chaos wrapped in silence. It spread softly, down the Swan's Road from the ancestral other-world, the epic North.

By stealth it drifted from weather forecasters' maps, crossing the land, covering fields, roads, woods, towns with a
persistent, anxious beauty.

Snow the terrorist: the more we fought against it,
the more frustrated we became. All our mountains of
grit couldn't protect us from the fragile delicacy of
snowflakes. Our society turned from winter like our
towns turned their backs on rivers. Talk of global warming
gave the lie to the return of the Arctic and we thought
the new Nature, bad as it's cracked-up to be, would rid
us of old Nature, whose powers gave birth to savage gods.
Now, instead of a southern season of sleeveless
insouciance, the old bastards were back: ice, snow and
freezing, silent chaos.

From the corner of my eye, I caught sight of a deer
running downhill through ash and hawthorn trees. It was
dark-backed and light-legged, its head high to see, hear and
smell across the white spaces in the wood. I couldn't see
anything chasing it but hunger would if it got much colder
for much longer. Perhaps we also remembered the
cold North breathing down our necks as we struggled to
carry on with what we pretended was normality.

III.

This swan-white world would soon be spirited away. The
snow that changed everything – covered the ground, dressed
trees and hills, brought a silent music and made the familiar
strange – would thaw. And when it did the green earth

would return as if the doors of a great cabinet had swung open and we see the Magician's Glamorous Assistant. She had stepped into the cabinet when the Magician tricked the world out with snow, and when it vanishes the Assistant makes a miraculous reappearance. In a funny way, we will be disappointed to see her.

Perhaps we are expecting a metamorphosis, at least some kind of change to the world that was covered in snow. Instead, there will be the same old Assistant, not quite as glamorous as when she disappeared, a bit flattened, damp, spoiled.

As the last of the snow melts into mud, the birds become agitated. With their flinty little calls and hesitant flitting there is little to distinguish them except for flashes of colour: the golden rump-spot of a green woodpecker leaving a mole hill because the ant mounds are still frozen; double white tail flashes of chaffinch flicker like lights in the hedge trees; red and white bullfinch, all blood and bandages; black stripe over yellow shield on a great tit's chest. The brightness of morning fades to silver-blue.

Warmer and sunnier now, birds pick up the pace. I pick up a stick from a pile of coppiced hazel and break the end off to fit it for the miles it has to do, stabbing squalid bits of puddle ice, ratcheting up steep banks to skirt the cliffs, poking about in leaf-mould. Ravens and buzzards are quiet, ghosting through treetops or brooding moodily down in fields or up telegraph poles. A kestrel hovers over a sodden meadow, poised between times.

The streams have got their chuckle back: intoxicated with snow melt and rain their yellow and blue scoured-clean beds shine under racing cold clear water and sound folds over little falls. On a bend of the brook there was a flash of white – the Magician's Glamorous Assistant rediscovers her smile – snowdrops.

IV.

Places can be found and lost. We traditionally think of them as being there: places are fixed reference points in the land-scapes of our physical and emotional geographies. That's so for some but many places are ephemeral or rapidly chang-ing. They can be brought by swans, by snow, by thaw. They can emerge from stories we tell and retell through the ages or from moods in which words mean nothing. They can barely exist at all before being swept away in a flood or they can have travelled through history with us only to be destroyed by our actions. Of course, many places are significant to wild animals and plants – we may stumble across them if we're lucky and leave them alone if we have the heart.

All these places – lost or found – are part of the language of the world. Whether they've been around for centuries or seconds, recognising them, giving them names, is a way we understand and live in the world. How we read these places and the lives which inhabit them depends on an ecological and cultural literacy that we've developed over a long history but which has become almost dismantled in recent times.

Our language and swans came from the same place, and yet we and the birds are so far apart now. Although the thrill of encounter still exists, it almost has to be reinvented, re-described in order for that emotional connection with the wild to find a purchase on modern culture. The words we use to describe things are also the way we value them. Destroy the language of places and we lose the places. When we lose the places, the wildlife of those places is lost too. Reclaim the language, reclaim the land, free the wild!

Wetwordland

I don't know what a *wetland* is. 'Land what is wet' doesn't really explain it. I think *wetland* is like *biodiversity* – a cobbled-together word in which 'biological' and 'diversity' are crunched up, squeezing out the 'logical' which makes its meaning opaque. Or maybe it's like *wildlife*, which used to mean the kind of 'life' which was 'wild', that is, beyond human governance, but by shoving those words together it became 'wildlife', the noun for that to be managed as a commodity for people. I worry that *wetland* is a catchall word, a sump where the poetry of water drains.

What about the burbling brook, beck, burn, bourne, stream,
    prill
What about the arterial rivulet, river, afon, meander, canal,
    waterway
And the drama of floods, flashes, washes, deluges,
    soddenings
What about upwellings of oozes, seeps, flushes, springs,
    wells, fonts, founts
And sublime tumble-downings of falls, cascades, torrents,
    pystill, spouts
What about the rude ditches, drains, dykes, flushes,
    channels, scrapes, cuts
The glittering lakes, llyn, lochs, meres, fens, broads
And the intimacy of puddles, ponds, pools, tarns, cwm,
    corries, pingos, flarks
And the dangerousness of swamps, sloughs, quagmires,
    swingsholms, marshes, mosses, bogs
What about trickles through soil into dark underground
    cave systems and aquifers
Or the saltings, mudflats, sandbars, foreshores of estuaries,
    rheas, fjords, deltas
What about all those soggy bottoms and damp patches I
    can't remember?

Don't pull the plug on the poetry of watery places; *wetland* won't do. We owe it to all their sopping, sloppy, soaked, sodden, muddy, mucky, mired, wringing wet and unreconstructed *wild* lives to call them by their proper names.

How to Tell the Difference between …

A Primrose and a Cowslip

When primroses (*Primula vulgaris*) and cowslips (*Primula veris*) are in flower then telling the difference between these two spring flowers is the essence of simplicity. Whilst the primrose has classic open flowers, the cowslip has a number of smaller, bell-shaped flowers attached to a stem held high above the plant.

However, when these two plants aren't in flower, identification becomes rather more difficult due to the similar appearance of the leaves.

But there is a way to tell the difference between the foliage of the cowslip and the primrose, and that is to look towards the base of the leaf. In primroses the leaf gently tapers down to a point, whilst in the cowslip the leaf tapers down far quicker, leaving only a very narrow area of leaf towards the leaf base.

How to See Wildlife

Colin Elford

It is not at all unusual to be waved down while driving along a forest track. The side window is normally tapped and as I wind down the window I find myself looking into the eyes of some excitable and often loud woodland walker. As a forest ranger I would need far more fingers and thumbs to count the times I have been asked, 'Where is all this wildlife? On the map we were given it says that you can see deer, but we never saw any, did we love?' the questioner would say, turning to his wife. Raising an eyebrow and trying to look surprised I start the conversation by asking the time. The questioner would then look blankly at his wife who would quickly roll back her sleeve, but finding the task awkward would stuff a dog's lead that was in her hand deep into her pocket. We would then both watch as the poor woman struggled to find her watch buried under layers of noisy waterproof clothing. 'Er, it's about twelve o'clock.' After hearing the time I would politely and slowly attempt to explain the life cycles of the local deer, and that they have differing hours of activity than our own, and that at noon most sensible deer are tucked up somewhere in a deep thicket away from us humans and our unruly dogs. At the mention of the word 'dog' the man's pupils expand. 'Oh yes,' he says, 'that's the other thing I was going to ask you. Have you seen a dog on your travels around the forest?'

Since man morphed from a rib or evolved from an ape, he has pursued fellow creatures of the earth, trapping and shooting them for food, or hunting them for the pure pleasure of the chase. Our wildlife has even been slaughtered for merely having the audacity to compete with us. So it should come as no surprise that animals and some birds have learnt to stay well clear of human beings. Finding and watching animals that would sooner not have us about is a difficult thing to achieve, especially if you lack even a modest outline knowledge of the animal or bird you intend to watch. But why try and invent the wheel when it is possible to learn from other people's experiences with wildlife through the pages of a book on the creatures you intend to watch?

Gaining good wood or field craft is a skill that takes years to build up while being out in nature. Don't worry if you make odd mistakes, for you will be in good company, but learn from them. There are a few things that are common sense when watching wild creatures. Firstly, wear drab silent clothing, keep quiet, always move slowly, and if you are using binoculars move your hands and face very slowly.

Wildlife notices any sharp movement, so remember, your aim is to allow creatures to come to you while remaining unobtrusive. This skill when learnt is a great gift.

I find it quite funny that even today people are still debating over that age-old question whether, heaven forbid, we could be animals ourselves, and not this noble creature that should have overall power over all nature. For what it's worth, I think that if we are not animals then we are surely only the width of a larch needle away, because our brethren on this earth appear to do identical things that we do: we all need to eat, drink and have familiar neighbourhoods to which we are tied one way or another. When you really start nature watching, practically any living thing can be absorbing; even a common bird such as the woodpigeon can make an interesting subject to study. Up close the colour is outstanding, that salmon pink breast, the metallic nape that resembles more fish scales than feathers, the gunmetal greys and streaks of pure white that flash in the blue of summer and light the smoky greys of winter. When watching wildlife one trap you should always try and avoid is to add your human stamp on what you see and make comparisons. Nature has been around a long time before we stumbled across it; far better to watch, listen and learn. Time is never wasted when watching wildlife.

Start your watching career with an easy subject, typically a bird or animal that lives near to you; read up on your chosen species and get a head start on the basics, like the type of habitat and food source they prefer. Watching wildlife as a hobby is a cheap pastime. You only really need a certain amount of knowledge to start and a set of drab quiet clothing which includes a hat. Hats of any shape break up your outline and take some of the glare from your face, as in bad light your face (and hands, incidentally) glows like the bottom of an upturned swede. I have found a good way to test yourself in remaining still and at the same time check the concealment ability of your clothing is to simply lean against a tree as a woodpigeon flies overhead, and note if the bird sees you and veers from its course.

My knowledge and experience grew from regular watching of a rabbit burrow. There is always something happening in and around a burrow. When new kits are born it is fun watching them play and sprawl out, relaxing in the sun at the mouth of the burrow – it is quite amusing watching a rabbit yawn. Rabbits are often very alert, which helps hone your stalking ability when you need to get close. Being a prey species they introduce you to many predatory neighbours, like foxes that pass pretending to ignore them, only to turn and charge the unwary down at great speed. Stoats often visit the burrows to hunt, panicking the residents. In deep snow one late February I witnessed the full fury of a doe rabbit fighting and finally chasing away two hungry stoats trying to snatch her young kittens; several attempts were made, one kit was even grabbed but dropped; all survived. Once at work I have watched several stoats carry rabbits that they have killed, twice as big as themselves. Nature can be unpredictable!

In my job as a wildlife ranger I have learnt as much about people as the wildlife I work with on a daily basis. From ecologists to species-specific experts it appears there are few folk truly tuned in to the woodland environment where habitats are alive with the sounds, smells and tracks of various woodland dwellers. Even working in the woods every day, favouring dusk and dawn, I am a long way from knowing it all, far from it. Each day I learn more, but I realise one sure thing: with nature, there is no sure thing.

Occasionally when I am asked to lead a group of people on a nature walk or deer-watching event, people often remark, 'Cor, you've got good eyes!', but really my eyes are no different than theirs, the only difference is that over time my eyes have honed into the environment, so that when I am looking for a deer I am looking for parts, rather than the whole animal. Experience has taught me to notice movement, like the flick of an ear or a swish of a fallow deer's tail. As I previously mentioned, wild animals prefer to remain hidden and are rarely at ease in an open area. They favour thicker cover where you are unlikely to see the whole of your intended quarry. Once when taking an Austrian client around the woodland for a morning's roe buck stalking, we rested and waited in a high seat overlooking a glade. Waving his pipe in the air he was the first to break the silence. In a hushed voice and smiling he said, 'You. You are like a fox.' I took his words as a compliment for my prowess in the forest, unless of course it was his way of telling me that I smelt! Sitting and waiting, I have always felt, is the best way to watch any wildlife, to let them come to you. That way the creature is not disturbed, acts naturally, and it can also leave the area undisturbed.

Walking around quietly – commonly known as stalking – is another way, but it is more difficult. There are ways you can help yourself in the observance of wildlife when on foot. Firstly, get up a little earlier than usual, as most animals are still active and feeding during the early morning or getting ready to retire to a secluded part of the woodland to sleep until the arrival of dusk, when again most movement happens. Another tip is to leave your dog at home. I have heard it said that a dog is a silent partner; my dogs come to work with me daily but accompany me stalking only occasionally, as they are far from silent partners. Dogs seem to deliberately search for the most parched, windblown leaves to walk through, or water to wade through; they would rather walk noisily across iced puddles, splitting them, than go around them on a cold still morning. Yes, I'm a dog man, but when searching quietly for wildlife I leave the dogs in the truck.

You have to plan your route when stalking any animal, so that the wind remains in your face. To have the wind in your back travelling ahead of you is a wasted effort, as your scent is carried forward towards anything that can pick up your smell and disappear before you even arrive. At times it will be practically impossible to maintain a correct wind position due to woodland eddies, but if you attempt this practice you will over time get better results and learn to read wind direction.

We all live in a busy, fast-moving, hurried world, so that if you want to watch wildlife while walking rather than sitting you may need to teach yourself to SLOW DOWN. It is a skill to walk slowly and quietly. There is no need to hurry to the next ride just to peep around the corner, as the wildlife might be closer than you think. Animals alerted by any sound that they are not familiar with, or if they catch a faint whiff of your scent mixed in the movement of the air, will stand and stare motionless, and if partially hidden will remain there as you pass oblivious that you are being observed. Remember, you are meant to be watching them, not vice versa! I walk painfully slowly, keeping to the ride edges, staying as much as possible off the centre of the track, stopping occasionally and listening. I learnt this technique from the deer I watch and stalk. At times I might cross the ride to avoid streams of sunlight filtering onto the path, as walking through bright beams enhances movement and can catch the attention of an alert animal, which will, quickly and unnoticed, melt away into the shadows.

Take time to pause, lean against a tree for a time and wait, watching for any movement. If you like to scan with binoculars, move your hands slowly, in a kind of slow motion so as not to attract attention. Flicking white hands about is like flag waving to wildlife. At times animals can be absorbed in what they're doing – feeding or courtship – and reading these situations I have been able to get close without disturbing them, watching natural behaviour few people get to see. Memorable sights of deer, both bucks and stags, battling and fighting, mother rabbits and deer risking their lives protecting their young from predators, and observing new births and deaths; these are all part of the natural cycle, happening every day, that I feel privileged to share in.

It is possible to find out what wildlife lives in your local park or piece of woodland without even seeing them. Animals may seem to be invisible at times but they do leave signs. While walking slowly you become far more observant; watching where you're walking you soon notice that you might not have been the first to have walked up the ride that morning; other creatures were about while you were in bed. An easy technique to study footprints, trails and imprints is to look for disturbed ground – crossing places, sandy river banks, water holes, even the moist mud around the lip of a puddle – these are the places secrets are given away. Small rodents and squirrels are attracted to water, as well as many birds and butterflies. Marks left by the visitors can be identified using a good field guide book at a later date. As your experience in tracking becomes greater, the signs will paint a picture that you can see and read, allowing you to interpret the visitation or event that has taken place. Tracking is puzzling and pleasurable at the same time, and although our talents fall very short compared to wild creatures, it's still fun. Fresh snow is a good surface to go out tracking. Snow comes in many differing forms, and fairly firm but dry is best. There are still a few experienced hunters that can tell at a glance whether an animal or bird was walking or running, trotting or jumping, but such skill takes years to master. For a beginner the snow is an aid which will highlight pads and prints, and expose the distinctive hoof of a deer.

In snowy weather I always look around trees with ivy to indicate species and numbers of animals. Deer, hares and rabbits love and seek out fallen ivy in bad weather. Bramble is another plant to study as it is an important winter food source for deer, especially for our native roe deer. To see if you have deer in your local woods check the bramble bushes. Deer have no upper incisors so that when they bite off the young shoots they tend to rip or tear the tender stem, leaving it ragged and uneven, rather than the clean sharp cut or slice made by a rabbit or hare.

Many species have territories, with invisible boundaries that tie them to that area. Deer will scrape part of sapling, and also secrete a musk or scent on the stripped stick to mark territory. This yearly habit leaves the bark white, bare and noticeable, showing us evidence that a male deer lives here. Foxes leave droppings (scats) mixed with scent on prominent objects like stones or even mole heaps to show their invisible routes taken every night. Usually near or close to fox droppings, it's worth checking for runs (tunnels). If the droppings are near any bramble, or close to a fence, often more clues are left – mud stains under or on the lower strand of wire or (a common find) hair caught on the bramble prickle or barb of a stock fence.

Badgers use the same or similar routes but their hairs are distinguishable by colour and texture: the fox is as red as its name and somewhat woolly; badger guard hair is darker and much coarser. Badgers use well-trodden runways, flattening ground and vegetation en route to their main sett. The homes of badgers are fairly easy to distinguish from a fox earth: foxes tend to conceal their presence, at least at first, unlike the badger who leaves large amounts of spill outside the entrance, broadcasting its presence. There are a few ways of identifying ownership and occupancy. Firstly, look for shallow pits on the main tracks leading away from the holes – badger clans use these pits as latrines. Badgers also like to change their bedding regularly, leaving bedding on top of the spill to dry. In the heart of the wood they use natural materials such as dry bracken or grasses. Closer to a field edge it is normal for them to use discarded straw which they bundle up between their front legs and drag backwards along their runs back to the sett. This task leaves a trail of dry litter along the route which is another indicator of use. Badgers are strong diggers and pull large rocks and lumps of chalk up and out of the ground. If you find fresh large heaps, especially on chalk, and you can see claw scrapes on the excavated material, then you can be certain it would be a good sett to watch as badgers would be very active there. You may find a sett that looks unused, possibly with entrances closed with cobwebs, so if you are unsure place small pieces of sticks across the mouth of the entrances and then check the site later for signs of activity. The more observant may even notice the claw marks on a nearby tree used by the badgers to clean their claws, and use as a scratching post and back rubber.

Winter when the snow is on the ground is a useful time to check on badger activity, as they bring mud outside from deep inside the sett on their feet, allowing you to track and study their nocturnal outings. However, it's late March and early April, before the bracken really shoots up, that I have found to be the best time for watching badgers. Sometimes during the day I might even cut a little vegetation to get a better view in advance of a night's watch. I have had some great fun watching badgers, especially the cubs. It is not unusual to have a badger cub walk over your feet if you are sitting stone still. Badgers may have brilliant noses but their eyesight is poor. The best night's badger watching I ever had was when I saw a half-grown fox emerge out of a large and very busy sett. The fox was not at all fazed by the number of badgers around the mouth entrance. Firstly it shook the dust from its coat, then, wrapping its brush between its legs like a scolded dog, it dashed between the jaws of the snapping badgers squealing with delight. Being nimble it danced smoothly between the circle of badgers and to my surprise the young fox spun around and returned back to its playmates for more frolics. I watched that fox racing back and forth for about half an hour, and when it finally tired I was convinced that what I'd witnessed was pure playfulness.

Throughout history the poor old fox has been persecuted, so that now in the country they select a site for an earth off the beaten track. A sure way of identifying an inhabited fox earth is to smell just inside the hole entrance. Dens that have only been visited leave a weak odour; a well-used one contains a strong lingering musky scent. Fox cubs, like puppies, love to play with anything they can put in their mouths, and bird wings and the remains of prey are often discarded around the den area, which is another pointer to the earth being in use. A word of caution: if you discover a hole in the spring with remains scattered about, do not go near the entrance or allow your dog to put its nose down it because a vixen with very young cubs will often move them if she feels her home has been discovered. When watching cubs it is far better to wait and view a good distance away, with the wind always in your favour. On approaching any sett or earth find a comfortable secluded place to observe from, but also select a quiet route away from the main holes when you depart. For the really serious watcher a collapsible, portable high seat which gets you off the ground is best. Placed against a convenient tree these seats offer safe, panoramic viewing.

You do not need a vast forest to watch wildlife. You can find wildlife in parks, estuaries, along river banks, on moors and mountains. With a little planning and a lot of patience even an urban garden, baited or set out to attract wildlife, can coax many mammals, insects and birds to your door. Heath land can also be places of interest. Reptiles live within the thick heather and dry grasses, making them difficult to locate, but in spring and autumn they can be found basking in sheltered sunlit spots. Mornings in the spring are the most productive times to start your search for them, creeping at slow pace; it's best to study the ground ahead as you walk. Reptiles are well camouflaged for a reason: they do not want to be found. A pause occasionally in the pace is a good system, as this allows your eyes to adjust. Lizards and snakes feel vibration through the ground, so it is a common practice when you are in training to scare off a reptile from its basking place; all you see is a fleeting blur disappearing into the nearest vegetation. When this happens, remain still and wait because there is a good chance that the snake or lizard will return back to the same spot. If I monitor reptiles I concentrate on the sandy strips on the ride edge, and also any of the south-facing heather slopes or secluded glades – all are of interest to these sensitive little creatures.

Nature watching is an encompassing subject too huge to put in a few words, but armed with patience, concern and care of the subject and a sprinkling of common sense watching wildlife is far from wasting valuable hours away. I believe it is good for you. In slowing down, nature can calm you, inspire and surprise, leaving you to appreciate and reflect on life and the small part you play.

Two Moors Walk

Martin Noble

B eing in a band generally involves touring great distances all over the world, sometimes through truly spectacular landscapes such as the Nevada Desert, the canyons of Utah, the Alps and the mountains of Taiwan. Being captive for such long durations, staring through the window at these magical scenes, can really drive you crackers. It certainly develops a strong urge to get out there, in amongst it. So, after finishing a lengthy spell of touring, I had a week off in early spring 2009, and decided to go walking in England with my girlfriend. We decided to walk the Two Moors Way (TMW) which crosses Dartmoor and Exmoor, 103 miles north to south, linked by the Exe Valley in the middle. The TMW traverses a variety of stunning landscapes including large stretches of open moorland, rural villages and deep wooded river valleys. Dartmoor also boasts more prehistoric remains than any other National Park in Europe, and Exmoor possesses a rich variety of wildlife.

We started in Ivybridge, South Dartmoor, and headed north to Lynmouth, on the North Exmoor coast.

Day 1) Ivybridge–Scorriton (14 miles)
SUNDAY 22 MARCH 2009

Having breakfast cooked for you is always a great way to start the day. Baked beans, toast, bacon, eggs and a nice cup of tea. Bellies full, bags packed and a clear sky above, we passed the old paper mill and headed out of Ivybridge.

A gentle ascent over fields and up stony paths led us to the edge of Dartmoor. From here, we followed the remains of a disused Redlake Tramway, which once served a china clay works. Out of breath, blood pumping and feeling good, we reached the top of the moor. With the cold wind blowing in my face, it instantly struck me how barren it was. Dartmoor was a desert of dried grass. No purple heather. No coconut-scented gorse blossom. The yellow blanket of moorland hay was a stunning contrast to the vast blue sky. Although seemingly lifeless, Skylarks climbed the air, trilling and chattering. Further on, a startled Snipe sprang up and flew into the distance. Within a couple of hours we were in the heart of Dartmoor, without a sign of civilisation. A heavily pregnant Dartmoor Pony wandered up to us for a 'chat' and a nibble of our food.

Our first sighting of Dartmoor's famous prehistoric remains was a stone row. Stretching 300 metres in front of us, it looked like a set of giant granite dominos waiting to be

knocked over. A Wheatear, looking like a masked highway-
man of the moors, led us down the track a few hundred
metres before retracing its journey and flashing its white
rump. (Its name refers to the prominent white rump –
'wheat' derived from 'white', and 'ear' meaning 'arse'.)

After some lunch, we descended into a valley where the
river Avon ran. Stagnant puddles lay at the sides of the river,
overpopulated with thousands of two-legged tadpoles,
standing on each other's heads, gasping for oxygen. This
part of the walk took us on a section of the 'Abbots Way',
which serves Buckfast Abbey. The monks there still make
'Buckfast Tonic Wine', a favourite tipple and 'badge of
honour' of Scottish underage drinkers. It was almost banned
in Scotland, prompting 'Don't Ban Buckie' demonstrations.
It was easy to imagine monks trundling through these
moors, tipsy, laughing and spilling Buckfast down their
tunics. At a ford further on a pair of Stonechats were
stationed on some mill ruins. Their striking tricolour plumage of orange-red breast, black head and white patches on
their necks was very clear at such close quarters. We stopped
and watched them feed, hovering, fluttering and dropping to
the ground to pick up food, before returning to the mill
ruins to eat their catch.

The final mile took us past two pot-bellied pigs in their
little mucky haven. They trotted over, snuffling for food and
a good old head scratch. On the descent into Scorriton there
were beautiful views across the valley to Buckland Beacon
and Rippon Tor. It was a lovely end to the day's walk.

We arrived at 5 p.m. as the sun was starting to set. Our B&B room was decorated in the 'country twee meets medieval boudoir' style, which was slightly bewildering. Over at the village pub we considered the next day's walk, which was six miles longer than today's. It wasn't yet British Summer Time, so to avoid walking in the dark we'd have to set off early in the morning. We raised our glasses of 'Jail Ale' to the nearby category C prison, HM Prison Dartmoor, and then headed back to our B&B. The night sky was full of shining stars.

Day 2) Scorriton–Chagford (20 miles)
MONDAY 23 MARCH 2009

After another belly-busting breakfast, we set off early. Outside it was grey and overcast. The first mile was a steady climb to the village of Holne. Beyond Holne, the TMW descended through fields into lovely oak and ash woodland by the side of the River Dart. It was a lovely change of scenery after yesterday's barren landscape. In an adjoining pond, the unmistakable rusty sails and whiskers of a pair of Mandarin Ducks caught our eye, looking like some ornate, oriental remote-controlled toys.

A steep winding ascent took us back to the top of the moor where the wind was blowing wildly. All along the moorland plateau were stunning views across the Dart valley, with the shape of the River Dart clear and pronounced through the leafless trees.

On the descent through Sherberton Common I saw my first ever Merlin. The elusive falcon rose from behind bramble bushes. Flying close to the ground, it gently glided back down amongst the ferns. It was a brief but sublime encounter.

A few miles on, a steep road took us out onto open moorland again. There are very few way-markers on the moors, so we followed sheep tracks uphill, northwards, towards the blustery peak. Masses of hay had become entangled in the gorse bushes, creating giant beehive-like structures all over the moor. It looked like a strange film set for an eerie episode of *Dr Who*.

Walking along the ridge, battling the wind for an hour or so, we eventually reached the Bronze Age heritage site of Grimspound. It's the most impressive and best known archaeological site on Dartmoor. The settlement consists of 24 hut circles surrounded by a low stone wall. We pottered around the ancient houses and then climbed up to Hookney Tor to gaze down on the mighty works of old and the great vastness of central Dartmoor. Desolate and deeply atmospheric, it's easy to imagine Arthur Conan Doyle's hellish hound roaming the land.

On Chagford Common, only three or four miles from our hotel, the footpath disintegrated into a number of sheep tracks. We followed the clearest well-trodden track for a while. It eventually led us into a dead end in the corner of a walled field. Confused, we checked the map and surveyed the surrounding contours. Fairly confident, we strode on, following what we thought was the 'Mariners Way' to Chagford. After walking down wildly overgrown paths, passing rotten way-markers and crumbling stiles, we began to have some doubts. We pressed on, through a creepy, run-down farm with an enormous tractor/car graveyard. We got the impression we really shouldn't be there.

Finally, we hit a road, though we had no idea where we actually were. Worse still, it had started to rain and the sun was setting. We took a gamble and headed up a winding country lane. Alarmingly we found ourselves walking out onto open moorland again. Darkness and mild panic descended on us. We agreed that going onto the moors at nightfall, in the rain, was not a good idea, so we turned back. By a stroke of luck, we bumped into a local man walking his black Labrador. He pointed us in the right direction. Chagford was three miles away by road. Exhausted and soaking wet, we marched along the road in twilight and silence. We were grateful when Chagford's streetlights emerged, guiding us to our hotel.

At dinner we realised we'd added at least four miles onto the walk by getting lost. We laughed, and then sighed, knowing we were due to do a similar distance again in the morning. That meant no sleeping in. Slightly crestfallen, we had a few beers and went to bed.

Day 3) Chagford–Morchard Road (19 miles)
TUESDAY 24 MARCH 2009

Waking from a deep sleep, I could hardly move. It felt like someone had filled me up with lead overnight. We groaned and laughed at the aches and pains. Truth be told, we weren't looking forward to another 20-mile walk.

Down in the deserted breakfast room, the cook greeted us with a long face and a big sneeze. I ordered kippers and scrambled eggs. He returned to the kitchen, coughing and hawking. Minutes later, the microwave pinged. The chef reappeared and plonked some anaemic kippers in front of me, with a side order of rubbery egg. It was awful; I ate it anyway.

Under the bright morning sun the ancient stannary town of Chagford was very picturesque. We meandered through the town, picking up pasties and cakes from the bakery, and some fruit from a tiny greengrocer's.

We hobbled out of Chagford towards the River Teign, where a brightly coloured Yellow Wagtail was endearingly scurrying along the river bank, picking up insects and frantically wagging its tail. On a little island in the river was a Peter Randall-Page sculpture, a large granite boulder split in two revealing intricate mirror-image carvings. Following the course of the Teign, a Dipper darted past us, close to the surface of the river, a blur of white and chocolate brown. A few hundred metres on we saw it again, perched on a rock in the river, bobbing up and down, and diving into the water for food. It's always uplifting to watch these lively little birds at work.

We soon reached the strange, angular Castle Drogo. Built in the 1910s, and made entirely of granite, it was the last castle ever to be built in England. Part fairytale castle, part concrete bunker, it looks like a house designed by England captain John Terry. Leaving the castle behind, the TMW took us high above the valley, revealing panoramic views of Teign Gorge. After a mile or so, we stopped for lunch in the pretty thatched-cottage village of Drewsteignton. We ate our Cornish pasties and cream doughnuts on a bench outside the village post office, once again reminded that food tastes so much better when you've walked for it. The sun still beaming down on us, we set off again, the first primroses of spring brightening the pathway. A mile or two out of Drewsteignton, a dual carriageway marked the border of North Dartmoor, and the passage into the Exe Valley.

Whilst less spectacular, this part of the TMW, between the two National Parks, was more rural, remote and unspoilt. We passed ancient hedgerows, farms in various states of decay, and countless breeds of sheep with new-born lambs. The soil had started to take on a vivid red coloration, created from red Permian sandstone. Many of these red fields were growing nothing but swedes. We discovered the motherlode at Clannaborough, home of 'Devon Swedes'. Tens of thousands of swedes. Crates upon crates of them. Where did they all go? Who, or what, eats all these swedes?

An amazing orange sunset was illuminating the terra-cotta-coloured soil, producing an almost Martian glow to the landscape. Mindful of yesterday's walk in the dark, we lumbered on beside streams, through woodland and across endless swede fields, arriving at Morchard Road around nightfall. We treated ourselves to a lovely big dinner and wine. Woozy and boozy, we retired, and were in a deep sleep by 10.30.

Day 4) Morchard Road–Knowstone (17 miles)
WEDNESDAY 25 MARCH 2009

After another amazingly deep sleep, and full breakfast, we set off. Today was dull and overcast, and a chilly wind was blowing. We were in good spirits, though, knowing that we'd walked over half of the TMW, and the longest walks were out of the way. Although it wasn't famed for its wildlife, we were grateful that this pastoral mid-Devon section of the TMW was gentler, with fewer climbs. The TMW in the Exe Valley uses ancient footpaths linking the villages of Morchard Bishop, Black Dog and Witheridge, passing through farms, fields and woodland. After passing through the lovely village of Black Dog we stopped for lunch by a stream, enjoying the sound of the bubbling water and cawing of Rooks overhead. A Wren was going crackers in a nearby bush, like a jumped-up Jack Russell barking behind a garden fence.

We passed many farms, in various conditions. There were some small, well-kept organic farms with chickens running around the place. On one particularly run-down farm we noticed a few sheep with limps, and the rotting piles of manure had tractor tyres and dietary supplement bottles stuck in them. Was this normal? Was it something to do with the workload and supermarket squeezes?

After 10 miles we arrived in the town of Witheridge. We had developed terrible Achilles heel pains and we thought of getting a taxi the rest of the way. To mull it over we stopped in the Mitre Inn, took our boots off, and swigged a few painkillers down with beer. Tipsy, warm and happy, we wished we could stay there all day. After an hour in the pub we decided against the taxi ride, even though we had concerns about walking in the dark again. As soon as we put our boots on the pain returned. It felt like my foot was in a vice. Even slackening my boots did nothing. The beer and painkillers made me care less, though. The TMW mercifully followed a road for a few miles, so we changed to normal footwear to go easy on the Achilles. On reaching Knowstone Outer Moor we followed a boardwalk upstream over a luminescent river, the psychedelic colour of IRN-BRU. With its wet grassland, heathland, bog and scrub, Knowstone Moor is a great place to see birds. We'd planned to spend an hour or two there, but due to our pub stop, the short days and the hobbling, we had to walk straight on through. It was almost dark and we still had a mile or so to go. The last bit of the walk to the village of Knowstone was on road, so we switched back to our trainers.

On arrival, we dumped our bags, scrubbed up and headed over to the only pub in the village, The Masons Arms. We had a pint whilst they laid the tables and brought us the menu, along with some complimentary plaice goujons. Looking at the very expensive menu it became apparent this was a Michelin-starred restaurant. After such a gruelling day, we ordered the whole shebang. We ate and drank like a king and queen. It was the best meal I'd ever had.

Day 5) Knowstone–Withypool (14 miles)
THURSDAY 26 MARCH 2009

The incessant drumming on the skylight woke me up. With protesting muscles and a fuzzy head, I forced myself out of bed and looked out of the window. It was absolutely pissing it down. We ate breakfast leisurely, hopeful that the rain would cease, but it kept falling. We put our waterproofs on, laced up our boots (reactivating the pain in our Achilles) and set off. It must have been bucketing down for hours as temporary streams were flowing down the steep country roads, and the woodland paths were waterlogged and muddy. In spite of this, it was still a pleasure to be out in heavy rainfall, with all the sounds and smells that come with it. At one point the heavenly aroma of wild garlic wafted from the banks of the River Yeo.

After another long, boggy ascent we reached the village of West Anstey. Here, a bright red letterbox peeked through a wall of thick ivy, and the ancient church stood stoically in the rain. We spent the next mile or so walking a steep tarmac road out of West Anstey. Advancing uphill, the downpour obscured the views, turning them into misty, soft-focus landscapes. At the top of the hill we saw the huge moss-coated memorial stone dedicated to Joe Turner, the inspiration and founder of the TMW. The memorial stone heralded the southern border of Exmoor. No sooner had we stepped over the border than we saw a herd of Exmoor Ponies huddled together, their double coats far superior than ours. Hardy little things.

Over half of the Exmoor National Park is semi-natural habitat, with limited human interference. Topography and vegetation are very diverse, ranging from steep rugged cliffs and woodland to natural moorland of heather and scrub. It has sheltered woodland and open valleys, with many streams and rivers. It is little wonder that Exmoor has the best wildlife along the TMW.

The rain finally subsided, and although the sky remained grey and dull the yellow blooms of gorse flowers brightened the place up. We'd really missed the magic of the moorland the past two days. We had intended to get some food at the post office at Hawkridge but it had closed down, so other than sticky sweets and biscuits we were without food for the rest of the walk. Leaving Hawkridge, the heavens opened again, lashing it down as we crossed open moorland. Descending through woodland, the trees gave us some respite from the worst of it, and eventually the downpour stopped.

We finally arrived at the beauty spot of Tarr Steps, the prehistoric clapper bridge (1000 BC) that runs 55 metres across the River Barle. It is made up of 17 huge stone slabs, weighing 5 tonnes each. Myth has it that the Devil built the bridge at Tarr Steps and still has sunbathing rights on its stones.

With patches of blue sky appearing, we followed the River Barle upstream through Tarr Steps Woodland National Nature Reserve, home to Red Deer, Dormice, Otters and the rare Barbastelle Bat. Our journey through the nature reserve was perhaps the best part of the trip so far. The reserve consisted of oak and beech woodland, with pockets of ash, hazel and sycamore. There was also a richness of mosses, liverworts and lichens. On the river a pair of Gooseanders appeared, the female resplendent in her reddy-brown '80s mullet. After a fleeting moment, these handsome diving ducks disappeared from view.

Further on, we saw our second Dipper of the trip. It put on a good show for us, repeatedly smashing a small fish on a rock. It went on for so long we got bored and left him to it. On the riverside path we watched Long-tailed Tits, Nuthatch and Treecreepers, and in the woodland clearings we saw Meadow Pipits, Green Woodpeckers and red-legged Partridges scurrying for cover.

Whilst walking the final two miles, the grey clouds completely vanished and the sun beamed its warmth down on us. As we approached Withypool, a Peregrine Falcon powered overhead. The day was getting better by the minute. The grass verges on the road into Withypool were brimming with glorious yellow daffodils, leading us all the way to our resting place.

Day 6) Withypool–Lynmouth (19 miles)
FRIDAY 27 MARCH 2009

Today we had to cheat a bit. We had booked our hotel in Minehead, and the last bus from Lynmouth was at 5.45 p.m. There was no way we'd catch that bus, so we booked a taxi ride for the first six miles to the edge of the moorland. Outside, there was a nip in the air. To the south there were patches of blue sky, and to the north it was overcast and heavy. The taxi driver chatted all the way, talking sombrely about post office closures, empty rural churches, young people moving away to cities, and house prices being driven up by rich city workers buying second homes. He became most animated whilst berating the latest health and safety laws which meant he could no longer do the annual tyre race down the river. He looked too old for this kind of caper, but he definitely still had life in him.

No sooner had we stepped out of the taxi, hailstones pelted down from the sky. As we donned our waterproofs the hail shower transformed into a snow blizzard. Setting off over the fields, the faint paths became obscured by the snow until the whole field was a blanket of snow. We couldn't see more than 50 metres in front, and had no idea which direction to take. We consulted our semi-ruined map and headed roughly in the right direction, laughing nervously through the veil of snow. Fortunately, we caught sight of the way-marker at the Exe Head crossroads which directed us north, into the heart of a snow-covered Exmoor. The snowfall morphed into light rain, melting the snow and opening up the dramatic views over Exe Plain and into the beautiful river scenery of the Hoar Oak Water Valley. It was the loveliest moorland scenery of the whole trip. Since the downpour, the streams were full and raging, and the landscape was both curvaceous and rugged. We walked past the famous Hoar Oak tree. At the base lay a sheep which had fallen down the cliff to its grizzly death.

It was still overcast and drizzling as we reached the moorland plateau of Cheriton Ridge, a great expanse of moorland with impressive broad views, even in this poor weather. We passed remains of ancient cairns and hut circles before reaching the village of Cheriton, where a cockerel broadcast our arrival. From here it was only a few miles to Lynmouth. Charitably, the rain ceased too. The final stretch of the TMW led us through more lovely riverside woodland, then high up through woods overlooking Hoar Oak Water. We climbed up through the gorse-filled 'cleaves', until we were 800 feet above the East Lyn river weaving through the valley below. The views over the precipitous sides of the ravine and across the valley to the sea were stunning. Gradually, the coastline came into view, and finally, the seaside town of Lynmouth.

We zig-zagged down through woods to a mossy tarmac path that led down to Lynmouth. At the end of the path was a commemorative stone marking the opening of the Two Moors Way on 29 May 1976, just four days before I was born. Weathered and covered in moss and lichen, the commemorative stone would no doubt outlive me.

We'd arrived in Lynmouth early and were just in time to board the 3.30 bus. As the bus was climbing the steep hill out of Lynmouth there was an almighty crunch and the vehicle ground to a halt midway up the hill. The driver looked back at us with an expression of regret and amusement. The bus was crocked. After a call to the bus company, the driver advised us we had to disembark and catch the next, and last, bus to Minehead at 5.45 p.m.

We spent the next two hours traipsing round Lynmouth, and had our first cream tea of the trip. In the harbour, a small fishing boat had a life-size dummy of Paul O'Grady in it. We walked up the East and West Lyn rivers, trying to imagine the great floods that devastated Lynmouth in 1952. A storm of tropical intensity created flash floods, causing the river banks to burst with such ferocity the water swept away a chapel, a row of cottages and a fruit shop; 28 bridges were destroyed, 38 cars were washed out to sea and 34 people died.

Flitting back and forth, we saw another Dipper on the river, walking head first into the river to catch a meal before darting back to its favoured rock, getting on with business as usual.

The Night Fisher

Jon Berry

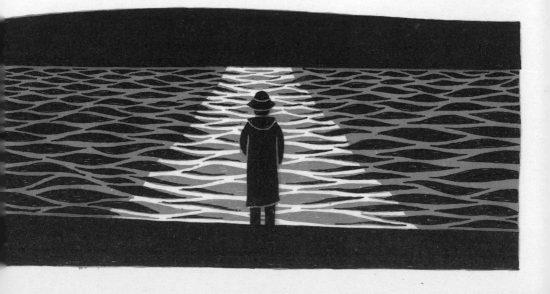

There is a moment at the end of each summer's day when the light falls off the horizon and stillness descends. If you are lucky enough to be away from roads, from towns and cities with their phosphorous polluted skies, far from the simian chatter of humanity, you can watch in silence as a familiar landscape disappears in shadow. Few of us notice this moment, but, when we do, it offers a serenity so profound that we are temporarily lost. For that captivating moment, the earth stands still.

Stalkers, foresters, countrymen – they know this moment. Lovers and poets know it too, in their own way. So too does the night fisher, the quiet, soft-treading soul abroad by water. It is this last breath of day, when the rivers and the lakes turn to black and the monsters awake, that he waits for. It is then, and precisely then, that the night fisher enters a new world of secrets.

For him, darkness means promise – of bites from fish too cautious to feed when the day-trippers are out, of giants who leave their hidey-holes only when the moon has risen. Night is the fisherman's secret edge, his chance to realise dreams that could never be fulfilled in the knowing glare of day. It can bring solitude too; the crowds who spend their day perched on wicker begin to melt away, towards their homes and suppers and wives, and the night fisher is alone.

Of course, there are fishers who camp by their waters, bivouacked and cocooned with sleeping bag and stove, with electronic devices to wake them when the fish arrive. Their night is lost beneath canvas and some of the magic is missed. These men are anglers and their only prize is the bounty they gather – they are not night fishers. No, the true example is the man who steps quietly out with rod, net and bag, protected only by an extra layer of wool and a flask – which may be thermal or hip, according to his taste. He prowls and stalks and listens for the ripples of moving fish, and when he hears them his hooks are baited in readiness. And then he waits, patiently and silently, for the stillness to break and the line to tighten. This waiting can last for hours, sometimes until the first moment of dawn, and he knows that on many nights his line will not move and the giants will not materialise. To all but the night fisher, it can resemble a kind of madness.

My brother and I began night fishing in 1984. The lake in question was a small monastery pool in the shadow of

Titchfield Abbey, a carp water with all the requisite mystery. It was intimate, reed-fringed and weed-choked, with elusive fish that knew better than to leave their sanctuaries in daylight. Brother and I tried many times to catch them between dawn and dusk, but we failed to do so. After a summer of indifference he and I knew that only the parallel universe of night offered us a chance.

We were woefully under-prepared for the first adventure. It was barely September, but the temperature in the early hours plummeted to a shivering low. Our torch succumbed to the cold and the damp, and the food was gone by midnight. The pool itself, which we knew so well in its daylight form, became a shape-shifting, unwelcoming stranger. Tree roots tripped us up, low branches scratched at our faces and the carp failed to appear. In the last hour of darkness my tiredness descended into a mild, hallucinatory delirium.

By dawn, when our father's Austin Maxi appeared at the top of the track to take us home, brother and I were bloodied and beaten. But we couldn't wait to return.

It was the first of many such nights. We persevered and caught some carp, and developed senses beyond those of our friends. We learnt to tread softly and place every footprint with caution and purpose, to feel our way through the darkness, to read the shadows on the water and tell instinctively where our baits had landed. We discovered too that nightfall brought a new lexicon of sounds – the scurrying of rats and water voles, the curmudgeonly shuffling of badgers, the heart-stopping shrieks of foxes. True silence was rare, but we were visitors in a nocturnal world and it would not stop just for us.

There were others who visited the lake in darkness and we came to know them well. All had a quiet, keen-eyed empathy with the surroundings, an ability to appear and disappear at will. Most were after the carp but there was one whose motives were less honourable. He was a poacher, a rabbiter who set snares in the fences around the lake at sunset and collected his lifeless prizes at dawn. We never learnt his true name and he would not have told us if we had asked, but one of his legs was wooden and so the night shift called him Jake. The step-thump-step of his approach was anything but subtle, but as a catcher of rabbits he was peerless.

Later, our school friends began to join us. We were glad of the company but they brought tents and torches and a sense of camaraderie that somehow shattered the spell. For the six weeks of summer, the pool became a campsite for a disparate band of O-Level survivors, and the carp and other animals retreated into silence. When the holidays ended and college beckoned, my brother and I were relieved to move on.

We found new places, pools and lakes we could haunt in the brief darkness of summer nights, and then left them in winter to explore the rivers. Eventually, we ventured down-stream to the coast and cast from deserted beaches into a sea whose waves reflected the stars. We found magic in a land-scape that could be sensed, smelt and heard. And we caught

fish: pike and perch, tench and eels, flounders and bass that
came ashore draped in weed and smelling of brine. If the
moon was full, every scale shone like a sovereign in the
palms of our hands.

I didn't forget about carp and returned to them when a
special water was revealed to me. The lake was large, thirty
acres or more, and though my friends fished there too it had
enough secret corners to accommodate us all. Like all real
carp lakes it had willows and lily beds, shallows and islands,
but it offered more besides. It sat among the lands of an
ancient country estate and there were follies and caves
hidden in the trees and a sunken arboretum on the southern
bank. The carp were ancient too, and – according to local
legend – shared the valley with a race of elfin folk known as
the mollies; the whole valley had a numinous quality, and
when darkness came and the mist descended it was like
following Alice through the looking glass. I never did see
one of the mollies and, despite countless nights of trying, I
never saw a big carp there either.

Some of the finest nights were devoted to trout. Just once,
I joined the sewin fishermen of south-west Wales, waiting
until the last light was extinguished before wading into the
Towy and casting flies for the silver fish that crashed through
each pool, fresh in on the evening tide. Fly-casting in darkness was, I soon found, an act of rhythm and poetry and
faith, and it was almost beyond me. I had to sense the exten-
sion of the line behind me, pause for the shortest of breaths
before pushing forward, and hope that all was well when my

leader fell into the black. I tangled and tripped and cracked off my flies in trees, but before the light came I had learnt enough to pull one fish from its waters. The trout was huge and beautiful and became the finest breakfast I have ever known.

On other occasions, I fished for sea trout and browns in the freestone rivers of the Highlands, waist-deep in water below a big northern sky. It was always too dark to see a rise to the fly and so I listened for the swirling vortex of a rolling fish and waited for the sudden pull of line over the tips of my fingers. Every bite came like an electric shock. When dawn came and I walked out of the river's valley into daylight, it was like leaving one world for another.

The sea trout men of Wales and Scotland were among the finest night fishers I have known. They arrived in darkness, their rods strung and ready, drably dressed in tweed and wool, each with a net strapped to their backs and a bag on their shoulders to carry their flies and flasks to the water. They spoke in whispers and cupped their hands to light each cigarette. Each knew that the foam of the river hid fish whose eyes were big and black and whose lateral lines were primed for signs of danger.

When the time came to wade into the water and begin their rhythmic poetry, it was as if the landscape absorbed them. They simply disappeared. Only the gentle, purposeful swish of their lines betrayed that they were there at all. This changed when a big fish was lost; there would be an audible curse and then a brief apology to invisible companions.

'Shit! *Sorry ...*'

'*Christ man, shhh!*'

'*Aye, sorry ...*'

And then heavy, guilty silence. The conversation would not have been out of place among the nightwatchmen of the Somme.

They were fine men, tough and profane but sensitive to the land around them. They understood the moods of the fish and had an empathy with the natural world that allowed them to read the moon, the wind and the water. Each could find his way among the boulders and rapids of the pools in inky blackness, and none carried a torch. It would have seemed an admission of failure.

But, like all night fishers, they knew fear. There were times when flood brought the river up and forced them to retreat, and when it happened they stood and smoked, watching tree trunks and sheep carcasses spiral downstream. On other occasions, lightning brought fire and light to the darkness and the men scurried up the bank to shelter. Every one of them had a story to tell of a night just like it and a friend who had fished on too long.

My own singular instance of bone-rattling fright took place not by the river, but on a glacial loch in the wilds of Sutherland. I was after the ferox trout that lived in its depths and, as the fish were proving elusive by day, I took out a boat at night. I was not alone, and my pal and I had no right to be afloat. The loch was twenty miles long and a mile wide, and fishing its bottomless waters in darkness was strictly forbidden. It was dangerous too, and so we taped a spotlight to the bow and kept a keen eye out for sudden rocks and shallows as we trolled its length. It was a cold and clear night, but that did not matter to us; it was the thought of capsizing that made our teeth chatter and our knuckles whiten. When morning came we were fishless, and we vowed never to do it again.

I am older now and rarely fish through the night. The first hours of darkness are enough to offer a chance and then I am gone, stealing away from the water while hardier sorts fish on. But, once or twice a year, dreams of monstrous creatures overpower me and I venture out with a promise to return when the sun has risen. I watch for the moment when the shadows claim the landscape and the ripples blacken, I listen as the language of the landscape changes and the cacophony of day makes way for the true sounds of the earth. But I am no poet. I am just a night fisher, and the moment is forgotten when the giants awake. I cast in silence, and wait for the pull that tells me there is magic at the end of my line.

How to Bird

Ceri Levy

One of the most frustrating things for me when I began bird watching was that I kept missing birds as they flew by or disappeared deeper into trees and foliage. My knowledge was limited and if I wasn't with experienced birders I really didn't know what I was looking at. I knew I had to learn some new skills that would prepare me for a birding life and that I had to improve and enhance the two tools of the bird-watching trade I already owned, my eyes and ears. Sight and/or sound will help identify a bird.

If you can't see a bird you can quite often hear it, and this gives the game away as to what may actually be lurking within a particular bush or tree. A birdcall overhead lets you know what is flying past. The three physical belongings one should have to help enhance one's abilities are binoculars, *The Collins Guide to Birds*, and a sound guide to calls and birdsong.

How to birdwatch

1. Find a bird and look at it through your binoculars.
2. Cross-reference the bird with your guidebook to ascertain what it is.
3. Learn the sound the bird makes.
4. Commit to memory. A notebook comes in handy to record sightings.

It all sounds simple really, but this is all one has to do to become a birdwatcher. But making these simple rules a way of life takes a lot of time and effort, and how good a bird-watcher one actually becomes is down to the amount of practice one puts into it. How to use your binoculars (often shortened to bins) is a skill that needs to be worked upon and speed of hand-to-eye coordination is invaluable in using them well.

I decided to learn how to become a better birdwatcher by using the limited views from my windows. I needed to hone my abilities at home, and what I practised there helped in my development as a birdwatcher.

Home learning

One of my first thoughts when I started watching birds was that I doubted whether there would be much to see living in the centre of London and that it was unfortunate that I didn't live in the middle of the country where birds were rife. I felt a hankering for the ability to look out of my window and to be able to watch birdlife. I live in a tree-lined street in a flat on the second floor; my front room looks out onto the street and the back of the flat overlooks rooftops and railway lines. I was pretty certain that not much would be living alongside me in this city chaos. And then I looked outside and started to watch … and to listen.

The first sign of birds is usually the sound of their calls and song. A key part of identifying birds is to learn the sounds of the common birds. For us townies, pigeons, tits, blackbirds, robins and wrens are probably, now, the most common bird sounds around us, and learning their songs and calls helps eliminate the common from the uncommon. There is no need to discover what the unseen bird singing in a bush is, if you immediately know the huge song of the minuscule wren. You hear another flurry of notes and know it is a blackbird buried in the garden hedge. The warning sounds of a robin click somewhere in the distance. Once you have learnt their language your time can be utilised better in searching for other birds and exploring the sounds you have never heard before. But learning by sound is a hard discipline as many birds have more than one call or song. A visual identification is sometimes easier as long as you can find and see the bird.

When I started watching from my front room window I noticed movement in the trees, but everything was moving too fast for me to ascertain what was flying through. By the time I had got hold of my binoculars, whatever it was that had rushed through my field of vision had disappeared. I knew I had to develop my skills and to learn how to read clues as to where and what type of birds were out there. At first glance it may seem as though there are only a few tits and pigeons, but the truth is that the more you look the more you see. And the more you practise your skills, the better your ability to see and hear birds becomes. They are all out there just waiting for us to see them.

Learn about movement and the difference between how the wind moves leaves and branches, to how a squirrel marches through them, and to how a bird flits between them. I watch common birds as they fly around the street, my learning centre. I study the flight styles of the blue and great tits and their neighbours. Then when I see a different movement and flight pattern I know I am on to something else. My first irregular visitor was a long-tailed tit, a bird lollipop with its huge tail topped by a little ball of pinks and browns. Learn the common, and the uncommon becomes obviously apparent.

Binocular practice is important and is akin to becoming an optical gunslinger. Speed of the draw is key to seeing birds. I learnt it at my flat window. I started practising speed of movement by looking at something inanimate such as a conker in the tree on the other side of the street and then trying to raise my bins and to focus them on it as quickly as possible. Not so easy, and it's not even moving. Look for a marker that can help you on your way to your subject. If you can see a recognisable large branch near your object of desire then try and find it in your binoculars and then you know you are in the right area to pinpoint your target. It's all about giving yourself a clue and finding something to latch on to visually, then there is a chance to decipher that whirr of colour into an actual bird. I still practise from my window. Any movement could be a bird. Practise and practise again. It helps, and some days a surprise awaits – such as the time a great spotted woodpecker suddenly appeared outside my window for five minutes, a common enough bird elsewhere but a first at home. If I had not been looking then I would never have seen it. It always makes me wonder how much passes by my window which remains unseen.

Once you have learnt a bird by its movement, its behaviour, its shape and its form, which in birding terms is known as its 'jizz', and you can physically and aurally recognise it, you are on an advanced path and it's time to get out there into the wild.

Moving to a location

Pick a location such as a nature reserve. There are going to be birds there for certain. Feel your confidence rise when you walk around and you know that what you can hear around you are blue tits and great tits. You have learnt their sounds and movements. But use your binoculars and confirm what you already know. Then you hear a sound you have not heard before. It's a bird up high, with a repetitive sound and a dry descending trill. You see a puffed-up pink breast. It is a chaffinch, your first one. Stay a while and learn his calls and song. It's another tick for your visual and aural senses.

A place you will learn to call home on a reserve is a hide. This is often a wooden hut with small windows or shutters built into at least one side of it to observe birds and wildlife from. Inside, time as we know it stops and the real world you have come from recedes from view and a bird-strewn picture continually paints itself in front of you. A hide can provide you with so much information because of the birds outside and the people who inhabit the inside. Degrees of expertise surround you in a hide, from the novice, which you are, to the seasoned veteran who has seen it all before. These people can become your teachers and your guides if they are treated properly. The majority of birders will impart knowledge for no fee. But there are ways to behave in a hide.

Remember to be as quiet as possible upon entry as people are concentrating and the birds can be easily disturbed by noise and the purpose of a hide is given in its title. Too much noise and you're no longer hidden. Once inside get a feel for the atmosphere and have a good scan with your binoculars upon the scene before you. Dig out the other essential part of your birdwatching kit, your *Collins Bird Guide*, and start looking up the birds you see outside and try to identify them for yourself. This is probably the most satisfying route to a higher state of bird being. But if perhaps you can't see anything outside or there is a bird and you're unsure of its identity, then don't be afraid to ask for help.

A simple question, which can and most often will elicit great information, is 'Anything about today?' The replies usually come packed with help. 'Not much. Some pochard, wigeon and a couple of snipe. That's about it really.' You may never have seen any of these birds and there are two ways you can go with the information you have just received. You can either immediately ask for help in identifying said birds or try and see them yourself. If you can't find them, then by all means ask for help. Everyone had to start off learning their birds some time and most birders will help out a novice. Of course, if the answer to 'Anything about?' is 'Yes, there is a bittern, which is showing well,' then don't be afraid to ask where the bittern is. Most of the time directions to the bird that awaits you will be given happily and often quickly. There is a satisfaction that comes with showing someone a bird they are keen to see and especially if it is a lifer (the first time you have seen a particular bird).

Of course you could end up with the person who decides to describe the situation of the bird in terms you don't understand. 'The bird is just to the left of the pittosporum, deep within the scrub and underneath the elder just to the left of the bladderwort.' You could reply, 'Thanks, but where in relation to the lone cow behind the reeds is the bird?' Sometimes, taking things down to their basest forms helps one find the bird. Learning to describe where a bird is in the landscape is important and the aim is that one day it will be you giving out the description, but one that everyone can understand. But it won't harm to learn the plants, shrubs and trees before you.

You can glean so much from talking to people as you wander around a reserve. Information is passed on as to the location of what birds are around, when they were seen, where they were seen, whether they are easy to see or difficult. Birders love to stop and discuss what's been seen, what should have been seen and what could be seen. It's a club that anyone can join and it's easy to take out a life membership.

Why should we bird?
Why should we care?

Birds can be guides to our world and to many of its inherent problems. Why did miners take a canary down a coalmine? Because it would be the first living being to become affected by any poisonous gases and would therefore become a warning to the miners of the imminent danger. Birds are one of the best indicators we have of impending trouble and we should take note of their plight more readily. If one wants to look at it selfishly, a crisis for birds is ultimately a crisis for man. If we take care of the birds we will be taking care of ourselves. Perhaps thinking of it in this way is the only way that we can engage more people in active support for conservation.

We live in an age of disconnection from nature, and birds have reconnected me to themselves and the world around me. Through them I have learnt more about the country and the earth I live upon than I have in all the years that they weren't in my life. They have led me down disused roads, to places I would never have visited before, beautiful locations as well as terrible ones, refuse dumps and idyllic refuges hidden away from the rest of the world. Through birds I have touched and connected with our land again.

Having birds in my life has filled a space that I never knew existed. Every day I see something wonderful, whether from my flat window or while out walking in the street, or at football, or while driving, or while shopping, or while …

Birds are everywhere. Just open your eyes, your heart as well as your mind and let them in.

To the Greenhouse

Tracey Thorn

I get a bit mystical in the greenhouse, which isn't like me at all. I'm very down to earth, hence my love of gardening, and a bit too sarcastic by nature to buy into an overtly 'spiritual' take on life. But I make an exception for this moment in the morning, at this time of year, when you go out with a coffee and step into the slightly steamy musty smell of the greenhouse and you wonder what will have happened overnight. The jobs that need doing really only take about five minutes, but once I'm in here I'm lost to the day. I'll stand and stare at a little pot which has a few green shoots pushing through, a pot which yesterday was 'just mud'. If you looked up in the kitchen, and glanced out the window and saw me there you'd think, 'What IS she doing?' and all I am doing is looking at it in wonder and thinking that most banal thought, 'It's a kind of miracle, isn't it?'

Kids, of course, can all be impressed by being allowed to plop a seed into a pot and then be shown it a few days later, a fairy-tale bean uncurling before their very eyes, but if you like gardening I don't think you ever grow out of that feeling of amazement. The prosaic fact that it WORKS, that what it says on the back of the seed packet will happen, does happen. That little bit of dried-up nothingness will turn out to contain an unstoppable force. And spring is the best moment of the gardening year in every single way. Everything is possible. All the leaves are long since cleared away, the veg beds are empty and dug, no mildew, no whitefly, no slugs. This year, yes THIS year, it will all go right, I will correct all the previous year's mistakes, and nature will be kind and smile upon my every effort, and it will all look like it looks in the books.

It won't, of course. I'll start out with the best intentions, and then get carried away. I'll be swayed by a picture and try something 'tricky' or something that doesn't really like my soil, or something that needs steady constant nurturing, not the binge-gardening approach that my poor plants get from me. Last year there were too few lettuces (slugs), too many cucumbers (ended up giving them away in the street) and some dahlia disappointment. But the carrots were hole-free, and the Cuore di Bue tomatoes were totally heart-shaped, and the courgettes and aubergines were great, and the mammoth basil was ginormous even if it did smell funny. I keep a diary of it all and note down the failures and successes and vow each year to learn from my mistakes and to become wiser and just BETTER at it all. And maybe I do, maybe I do, but after the neatness and perfection and possibility of spring I know enough now to know that it will all get messy in the end and nature will do whatever it bloody wants to, despite me.

Perhaps it was a mistake trying to grow 'La Diva' cucumbers.

They're sulky little madams at the best of times, cucumber plants. The slightest chill breeze, or a splash too much water on their feet, and that's it. They freeze you out, first by standing there looking you in the eye and REFUSING to grow another inch, then tossing their hair at you as they wilt slowly down into their pots. 'SEE! See what you've done to me with your neglect and cruelty ... oh, I die, I DIE!'

Last year I won them over. It was a project, albeit a slightly demeaning one, and I was at their beck and call every minute of the day for the first month or so; opening and closing the window on request, pulling down the blind at midday, fanning them, fetching a little muffler in the evenings. And I was rewarded with a glut of cucumbers the like of which I never wish to see again. Ended up literally GIVING them away. A box outside the house said, 'Help Yourself! Free Cucumbers! Take One! Please, Please Take One, No, Take Two, Wait, Come Back ...'

This year I have of course been slightly busier, so yes, a minuscule degree of neglect has crept in. There was one day when it got too hot in there, I admit, and possibly an evening last week when the temperature dropped a little lower than I would have liked before I remembered to shut the door. And the variety I'm growing this year is – La Diva! So I have lost two out of the three plants. And lost them in a Tallulah Bankhead-worthy performance of suffering and decline. I am not going to rise to it. I have sown four more, and they are already through.

Meanwhile, outside the weather has been changeable, in a way that is always alarming to gardeners; but I've already sown carrots and lettuces, and planted out beans, tomatoes and, today, the dahlias. It was a bit warm and muggy out there, slatey grey clouds, and while I was digging it suddenly became very very still all around me, the way it does when the wind drops just before it properly rains. A strange, indefinable kind of stillness, but not quiet, as it was filled with the sound of hidden birdsong from every tree, all alerting each other to the change in the weather that was coming, and the promise of worms. Peaceful and busy at the same time.

This year, for the first time ever, I visited Chelsea Flower Show. An evening event, to which I was invited by a friend who works in PR, meant that I was able to avoid the thronging daytime crowds, and scoot round the whole extravaganza in about an hour. A few random celebrities were dotted here and there in amongst the imported olive trees and the artfully arranged garden bric-à-brac. Rory Bremner over there, Britt Ekland over here, and up there Nicky Haslam, picking his way along a note-perfect reconstruction of a Provençal gravel path towards a lady in full evening dress playing the harp. It was, to say the least, incongruous, and whilst I had a thoroughly enjoyable evening, glass of champagne in hand, the impression I took away with me was that the Chelsea Flower Show has really sod all to do with gardening as I know and love it.

A couple of weeks later, I noticed in *Time Out* that it was the Open Garden Squares Weekend in London. Various green spaces – some well-known, some small and insignificant – were open to the public, and spotting one very near by, I announced on Sunday afternoon that we were going to visit the Branch Hill allotments in Hampstead.

In many ways it was a classic family outing – the weather turned too hot as we traipsed up the hill, it was a little further than we thought, the oldest kids moaned about the distance, and the youngest, wearing new Crocs for the first time, got blisters and had to be revived with a bottle of Oasis and a pack of plasters. But when finally we got there, it restored my faith in the wonder and beauty of gardening, and made me feel again that it was something anyone could do, and could then share with anyone else who did it. There was that combination of the ramshackle and the orderly common to all allotments, and which I love more than any sweeping lawn or herbaceous border. Neat rows of yellow-stalked chard, carefully netted raspberry bushes, diligently earthed-up rows of potatoes. All interspersed with home-made, *Blue Peter*-style garden contraptions – slug traps made from yoghurt pots with an inch of beer at the bottom,

CDs tied to bamboo canes, fluttering and glinting in the breeze, a low wall made of a random assortment of bricks and more or less square stones piled on top of each other. Even a semi-open greenhouse, which was just four half-height plyboard walls, and then some clear corrugated plastic above, but inside, basking in the warmth, a lush collection of tomato plants and strawberries.

What I realised was that there is a DIY quality to allotments, which reminds me of the atmosphere of the indie record scene that I grew up with. It's a bit rough round the edges, a bit alternative, but at the same time extremely industrious. There's an atmosphere of people working hard, and trying their absolute best to make things happen, but accepting all the imperfections that come from doing it yourself, as an amateur, rather than getting the professionals in. Still, I have to confess that I experienced this epiphany alone in our family group. The kids were patient enough, bless them, as they tried to fathom the reasons why I would want to look at someone else's beans when I have my own growing at home, but finally my nine-year-old came up with an analogy that was the only way he could make any sense of it – 'This is like Lego for you, isn't it, Mum?'

My mum sadly died at the end of July, and in the weeks running up, and the weeks following, I wasn't really up to doing anything much, let alone writing about my vegetables.

For the last three years I've done the plant stall at the school summer fête. It started as a casual suggestion in the playground, and then snowballed into a labour of gardening love which now dominates the spring and early summer for me. Basically, whenever I'm sowing seeds I sow some extra, and pot those things on to sell them at the fête. Tumbling Tom tomato plants, courgettes, aubergines, sweet peppers, basil, window-boxes of salad leaves, cuttings from my scented geraniums – I end up with about four car-loads of stuff to transport round to the school. But this year might be my last for a while, as the thanklessness of the task has begun to defeat me.

Like a dog-breeder reluctantly handing over puppies to a neglectful-looking owner, I hate selling my plants to people who so clearly are going to kill them.

'This courgette plant,' said one parent to me brightly, pointing at the lovely flower-tipped fruit balancing on the edge of the pot, 'will it have any MORE courgettes after this one?' Probably not, in your hands, I stopped myself replying.

A teacher toyed with one of the tomato plants. 'So, at the end of the summer, do I just cut it down to the ground, and it will come up again next year?'

My favourite this year was from the archetypal hard-to-please north London mother. I'd never seen her before, but she came and stood in front of the plants, fingering them all disdainfully. Finally she deigned to speak to me. 'Tell me,' she said suspiciously, 'where do all the plants COME from?'

clearly suspecting that some kind of non-organic scandal was being perpetrated here in the name of gardening for charity.

I think next year I will take a break, and just run the tombola.

Anyway, that was back in June, and from July onwards, as my mum fell ill, the garden inevitably got neglected. The dwarf French beans became infested with blackfly, beyond the point of being controllable, so I left them to it, managing to pick only one colander-full of beans. They were beautiful once I'd rinsed and scraped off every single sticky black bug, but the sink afterwards looked disgusting, the site of a blackfly massacre. Some of the lettuces were left to bolt, and the tomatoes were underfed, so the leaves now have a yellowy drained appearance, and look about as appealing as a pair of stone-washed jeans.

But yes, there have been moments when the pottering round the garden, doing little jobs here and there, and watching things carrying on with their cycle of growing and producing has been as consoling as you'd expect. We've eaten lots of lovely things made from varying combinations of courgettes, aubergines, tomatoes and basil, to the point where possibly we don't actually WANT to eat anything else made of those things for quite some time.

And now the late summer decline has begun, and the inevitable downward curve towards winter seems right and proper this year, when my mind, of course, is occupied with thoughts of endings.

* * *

Oh, but I am a fair-weather gardener. I hang my head in shame as I tell you this, and I accept without complaint the accusation that it relegates me to the category of Not Really a Proper Gardener At All. But what can I say, it's the truth, and I have to own up to it here, if nowhere else.

At this time of year I embark on a grand and thoroughly self-defeating project of Putting Everything Off. The autumn clear-up needs to be started, I know it does, and I know everything will look better once I get on with it, but still … I fanny around making another cup of tea, I leaf through the paper, I go and make a stupid joke on Twitter … ANYTHING rather than dig up the mouldy courgette plants, haul the old grow bags out of the greenhouse, and generally start putting everything to bed for the winter.

This year my laziness is compounded by another fact, which is that of probable and imminent house-moving. There is every chance that by next spring we will be living in a different house, where I will have a much smaller garden and no greenhouse at all. You might think this is a nightmare haunting my every waking moment, but in fact I'm very excited about the move. I'm looking forward to the general down-sizing it represents, and I love the house we're moving to, but it does mean I have to think about saying goodbye to this particular garden. My heart is NEVER in the job of tidying up at the end of summer, because I am basically a) lazy and b) untidy, but this year I will be tidying up in order for someone else to start reaping the benefits next spring. And that someone might not even be much of a gardener. Might not want to grow vegetables. Might not even want my greenhouse.

Again, I stress that this really is not making me enormously sad. Despite a career of writing songs which suggest otherwise, I'm not a great dweller in the past, and once I've moved from anywhere I very easily leave it behind. But the mental energy that I would normally be putting into planning next year's seed-sowing and vegetable rotating I am now putting into the entirely different project of working out how I am going to garden in a much smaller space. I'll have to return to doing a lot more container gardening, which I love for its manageability, and without a greenhouse I'll be making use of indoor windowsills, and sheltered sunny corners, and possibly a cold-frame or two. I've started searching out the on-line blogs of those who manage to grow vegetables on the balconies of high-rise flats, and the economies of scale involved in this kind of project are just what appeal to my instinctive minimalism. I love the thought of having to make every square inch productive in some way, and am already envisaging beds which will have lettuces interspersed with flowering plants, and pots of herbs and tomatoes which will look as ornamental as the geraniums and hostas they will sit beside.

More than anything, what excites me is the prospect of change. In truth, gardening can become repetitive, the same jobs need doing at the same time of year, every year, and whilst that is one of its comforts and pleasures it can occasionally lead to a loss of inspiration. A new space, even a smaller one which will inevitably place restrictions on what I can do, contains new possibilities, and new problems which have to be solved. Planning is required. Much consulting of books for ideas. The studying of other people's gardening blogs … it's all VERY VERY IMPORTANT AND TIME-CONSUMING and means I can't go outside and clear up those dahlias just now. Sorry.

Hidden Truth in the
Lie of the Land

Ian Vince

I spent an hour or two barrelling around the monadnocks of Sutherland in a postbus once. It was a bright
March day, with a fresh covering of snow and I was on
my way to the North-West Highlands, heading towards not
only the top left-hand corner of Scotland but also the most
ancient part of Europe where the rock is up to 3 billion
years old. That was the day I realised that every landscape
has a way of explaining itself.

One of the epic landscapes of Britain, this part of Scotland was, until relatively recently, attached to the Canadian
Shield – the geological nucleus of North America. And,
aside from the wild antediluvian overtones of the hummocky
plateaux around Loch Assynt – an ambience that suggests
you might suddenly encounter a herd of herbivores, each
the approximate dimensions of a parish church, around the
next bend – there is also a transatlantic otherness about the
place. Indeed, on bright, snow-bound days the landscape

still wears an American smile; everywhere gleams toothpaste white in a glaring, razor-thin sunlight, with only silhouetted fence posts and the odd lone stag standing out as details in a minimalist tableau. On that day the landscape was reduced to its absolute bare essentials – all grand lines and sweeping curves under an arching blue sky – as Donald the postbus driver managed to share an observation about the snow between light-hearted tales of life in adversity in the Highlands. His observation, which was accompanied by a mischievous twinkle in his eye, was that 'snow reveals more than it conceals'.

To be fair, on that particular day it was really the only way of looking at things, especially the larger-than-life vistas of the North-West Highlands – a landscape formed when one slab of crust was pushed and thrown forty miles over another. A challenge to the view that Britain's scenery is no more than a foothill to the world, these mountains are of a scale and sublime grandeur that reflects their ancient origin as Himalayan behemoths of the first order. The mountain prospect is home to such little detail that the impact of the scenery is only enhanced by snow. On a wet day in November they can appear unadorned, stark and unforgiving – like the scenic equivalent of your local tax office – but under alpine conditions every arête is honed, every corrie is picked out in the light and the whole thing gleams like a drawer full of knives.

Elsewhere, the landscape is usually more subtle but no less exotic, and always reveals something about itself in the viewing. At various times in the long history of these islands Britain has seen Namibian-style deserts, volcanoes of a Krakatoan disposition and tropical, cerulean seas, not to mention mile-high glaciers, continental collisions and apocalyptic earthquakes. While all of this is now safely tucked away in the glory of Britain's past, each has left a legacy of tell-tale signs that can help unearth the deep history of an area, so that often, rather than the grand lines of escarpments and brutal overtones of a mountain range, understanding the landscape starts in the intimate details of the countryside around you.

Beech and ash trees, for instance, love the well-drained, thin and light soils found over chalk, and many a ring of them stand crowning a prominent down. A few years ago I camped with a clear view of Chanctonbury Ring on the South Downs in Sussex. It was Lughnasadh – the pagan equivalent of a 'harvest festival', only without the rusty tins of pineapple – and I watched the swing and bob of lanterns from a safe distance as witches danced around trees set on top of a vertiginous scarp slope every bit as forbidding as their moonlit escapades. The scarp of the South Downs stretched east and west like the hanging wall of some great tear in the landscape.

The South Downs rise to little more than 800 feet yet, from a perspective afforded by the various country roads which follow the bottom of the scarp slope along its length, they have the visual authority of a mountain three times their height. The gentler dip slopes of the escarpments follow the dip of the chalk beds, rucked up like a rug by the same collision – of Africa into Europe – responsible for the building of the Alps. Twenty million years ago the North and South Downs were connected by a giant arc of chalk, a super-down that stretched from Hampshire to Agincourt, a wide, green bridge the height of modern Snowdon along its crest. Most of this chalk has now been washed away, leaving only the limbs of the arch, the 800-foot-high stumps of the North and South Downs on which humans now dance on high days and holidays, desperately seeking some arcane source of power from the Earth. Perhaps they should be careful what they wish for.

Witchcraft notwithstanding, humans have long harvested what they can from the land beneath their feet, but this is particularly so with regard to building materials. The chalk of the South Downs, for instance, is far too soft and friable to be of much use for construction, but its beds contain regular layers of large knobbly flint nodules which are to chalk what diamond is to candyfloss. Flint is super-hard, whereas even a soft spring rain will eventually turn chalk the same way as an Alka-Seltzer on a grumpy Sunday morning. Flint – made from a fine-grained variety of quartz – and brick (probably baked from local clay) are used for a lot of the vernacular architecture on the chalk downs.

The built environment is littered with clues to what lies beneath. Nowhere is this more apparent than in the Cotswolds, where whole villages are made of a golden lime-stone known by geologists – in what sounds like a rather dismissive tone – as the Inferior Oolite. Its particular golden hue, evocative of sepia postcards and all things cosy and old, conspires to make many a Midlands village look as though it was constructed from a collection of enormous hollowed-out loaves. In the fields, the oxidising iron found in the limestone that creates this Hovis-grade nostalgia renders the soil a peculiar orangey-brown, rather like the aspirational 'gold' label coffee brands some of us bought in the 1980s, when our aspirations were that much more modest. Away from the country fields, Cotswold limestone reaches the apotheosis of its expression in the Great Oolite – the Bath Stone used for high-status buildings from the Royal Crescent to Oxford colleges – and its warm tones come from the same oxidising iron as the Inferior Oolite that has built thousands of Cotswold cottages.

At Dawlish in Devon iron oxides colour the cliffs that Brunel's Great Western Railway runs around, darting in and out of tunnels and arches framed with New Red Sandstone, a vibrant carmine that rivals the terra rossa soils of the Mediterranean, while the fertile local fields get their ochreous hue from the same source. Close inspection of the cliffs around Dawlish reveals another aspect of Britain's deep history; you can clearly see the cross-sections of ancient desert dunes from 200 to 300 million years ago, when Britain's climate was like that of modern New Mexico.

Inland, the tors of Dartmoor, Bodmin Moor and every eminence but one to the toe of Cornwall offer the traditional granite upland of poor peaty and acidic soil where heather thrives. But one Cornish moor is different. Goon-hilly Downs on the Lizard Peninsula is the only place in Britain where Cornish heath, *Erica vagans*, thrives. Unlike every other member of its largely lime-hating family, which includes rhododendrons and bilberries as well as heather, Cornish heath loves alkaline soils and the Lizard has them by virtue of a slab of oceanic crust which was unexpectedly thrust over the top of continental crust by a 400-million-year-old geological sleight-of-hand too rare and exotic to go into here. Even a geological map of relatively low detail shows the Lizard Peninsula as a riot of colour, as if geologists became suddenly influenced by the work of Jackson Pollock and abstract jazz.

Much can be found out about your local landscape from maps, but a detailed geological sheet is not necessary; a 1:50,000 Ordnance Survey Landranger map of the area is ideal, but even one of low detail, such as a road atlas, can serve well in finding some features of the landscape that may not be immediately obvious on the ground. Place-names can provide clues to the geography of an area – many of them explicitly mention topographic features like fords, fields, downs, islands, headlands and streams in Old and Middle English, Old Norse and the indigenous languages of the Celtic nations. A little bit of research can reveal interesting facets and long-forgotten facts about a place, all from its name. The Cornish name for St Michael's Mount – *Carrack Looz en Cooz*, the 'grey rock in the woods' – reveals that, far from being a few hundred yards offshore in a bay, it was once miles inland in the centre of a forest. Nearby fossilised tree stumps peek out from the sand and the dating of them confirms that a rise in sea levels towards the end of the last glaciation was responsible for miles of coastal inundation.

Place-names that feature the element 'bourne' or 'borne' in them usually indicate a stream or spring found in chalk and limestone landscapes. You may find villages named 'Winterbourne' – which is a stream that only flows in winter, a particular feature of a chalk landscape. Chalk is porous but in this country most of it rests on an impermeable layer of clay and rain drains through it and along the top of the clay until it reaches the surface as a spring. When winter rainfall raises the water table within the chalk, springs may appear further up the slope. When the water table drops again during the summer, the winterbourne dries up and will leave a dry valley behind. Other dry valleys may be shown on the map or feature in place names as 'combes', glacial features formed when summer meltwater rivers cut valleys into frozen ground, the one time when chalk is no longer porous. It's all a long way from the circumstances of chalk's original formation, built from billions of smidgens of microscopically small shells that settled out of a very warm cerulean sea around 80 million years ago.

You can go so far with maps, but for all our modern preoccupations with measurement, mapping, cataloguing, codifying and tabulating the landscape, as if beauty was in the eye of the auditor, our ancestors were way ahead of us if what they left behind is anything to go by. They seem to have had an innate understanding of landscape – or, perhaps, better spatial sense – than us. It's possible that we have lost something in our relentless lust for reductionism; maybe we can no longer see the landscape as a whole but only as an assemblage of imperfectly understood systems.

Stonehenge is the perfect example. We focus on a mysterious ring of stones and forget the landscape around it. The world-famous circle is positioned on an eminence in the landscape – a crown upon a topographical skull – in a way that suggests its builders were not satisfied with merely erecting a temple, but wanted to manage participants' reactions to it. Set some way back from the brow, the henge is hidden from view along The Avenue, the ceremonial route from the River Avon a mile or so to the east. In a piece of pure theatre, Stonehenge becomes visible only on the final approach, where it appears to climb from the horizon like the midsummer sun.

An understanding of the landscape may have been what kept our ancestors alive at times; a better understanding of it now might help us with the problems we have been ignoring since we attempted to disconnect ourselves from the natural world in the grand übermenschian gesture that was the Industrial Revolution. Going to the North-West Highlands was a way of feeling the brute force of the landscape again and removing the human reference points. The pillar-like summits like Suilven that rise in an imposing fashion from the hummocky plateau seemed to sum up the prehistoric appeal of the place. Formed 3 billion years ago, disinterred, then buried again 2 billion years later, when there were still no complex organisms on the planet, then whittled and gouged away by glaciers to reveal the ancient landscape again, they ooze with the kind of menace completely absent from our modern lives. It is a landscape looked over by odd-shaped mountains – inselbergs or monadnocks like Suilven – laid down when even the dinosaurs were a distant and unlikely possibility.

Deeper than
the Wind

Dexter Petley

I.

We scrumpers knew our apples, the way a fence knows a pearl. It was a crime of nature encouraged by parents fond of proverbs. If money didn't grow on trees, fruit did. Beauty of Bath in the vicar's garden, Worcesters in the village orchards.

We were more than the pikey tea-leaves the parlour maid would take us for; we were four-season foragers, scrumpers by day and poachers by night. A bucket of eels from Risden, a buttered trout from Lord Millet's pool. Bucolic thugs maybe, whipper-snappers in the wheat, hop-garden hoodlums; our parents were grateful for the extras, and we carried an assortment of blades with their blessing – pocket knives for the whittling crafts, the topping and tailing of game, the bone-handled sheath knives for playing split the kipper.

We were Kent boys, the wild life of the Wealden shires. Field craft had scant intellectual rigour; we were born into it like cubs with the dirt round our eyes, dirt which came off Sunday nights in a tin bath and a boiling kettle. Our pockets were full of string and hops, chestnuts, rose-hips, rabbit tails, sheep's teeth. Our heads measured time in tench bubbles and cuckoo spit. We carried home-made weapons tucked into our belts; catapults cut from ash and hazel prods. A good shot meant rabbit or pigeon pie. Thus we hunted, killed and scrumped, knew our birds eggs, carried our bottles back to the shop, ironed brown paper bags to wrap our apples, played our games with common weeds, found our sweets in peapods and wheatears. Childhoods financed by the hedgerow fund; children built out of scrap. More marvellous than this, scrap had its own school.

The County Rural Secondary Modern School for Boys is condemned by historians of education as blazer borstal, employment for post-war chalk-Hitlers and purple colonels who drilled pupils devoid of academic ambition. The last of the rural moderns was closed in 1971 to make way for the plastic age, a comprehensive system for the inculcation of middle-managers, O-level check-out girls for the new supermarkets or pen-pushers who drove brown cars up the A21.

Swattenden School still stands in its 27 acres, a moderately austere early 19th-century mansion, whitewashed grey and window-taxed blank, ironic in its reincarnation as a Kent County Council environment and nature study centre.

In 1967 it was a repository of the de-selected scrap, the 11-plus failures. Few of us felt any bitterness on being sent there, for this was natural selection. We were the good-bad boys from the village farms and woods whose education was a curriculum of locality. No global village ambition, no equipping us for the wider *world* of work. We were educated along organic furrows, as if rural succession was a permaculture, not a threatened sociology. The object was realistic, community related: to sustain the life of the village as our elders knew it. To feed the farms and crafts that in turn fed us. My fellow classmates were from families as Wealden as weatherboard; fruit growers, dairy, meat and hop farmers, stockmen, hop pole turners, egg packers, foresters and tree surgeons, nurserymen, cricket bat makers, tractor mechanics, growers, mowers and breeders, cider makers, saddle makers and gamekeepers.

School houses were aptly named Brook, Dean, Hurst and Weald, and the school badge on our blazers was the crested crane of the nearby medieval cloth mill village of Cranbrook. The A, B and C streams flowed into Swattenden from natural springs bringing a flood of country wisdom to the pool, from Sandhurst, Hawkhurst, Cranbrook, Sissinghurst, Frittenden, Benenden, Goudhurst and Staplehurst.

It was the greatest event of my life, failing the 11-plus in 1967. It kept me out of grammar school town, confined within the landscapes I knew, among recognisable accents cut from thickets and hay bales, not from the prep and band box perfumes of the county set. In fact, it kept us out of history altogether. Today, the rural county schools are all but forgotten, remembered as failures, runts tied in a gunny sack, tossed long ago into a dark pool of rural reform.

The 1944 Education Act gave the rural secondary head teachers complete control of the school curriculum. Secular instruction, as they called it, was a matter for the LEA and the schools themselves. The Minister of Education had no legal right to determine the content of our education. This left instruction at the mercy of local conditions, regional employers, preparation for a locality then known as The Garden of England. In 1960, the minister, Sir David Eccles, admitted that it wasn't his place to enter 'the secret garden of the curriculum'.

And secret garden it was. We took our trugs to school and learnt to mix all six John Innes composts in the first year. Slackers were put to washing flower pots, and if you couldn't recite the ericaceous compost creed of 2 loam, 1 peat, 1 sand, you were sent to the school pig sties to weigh the weeners. Our gardening masters smoked pipes in the potting shed, had names like Mr Field, wore brown Bladens on hot summer days and somehow, because we were teenage hoodlums remember, organised us efficiently enough to grow the school's food.

I like to think that even now, forty years on, each tuber I plant goes into the ground because of Mr Field's doggedness. I was not his best pupil, but he taught me chitting well. As I write, hundreds of tubers are chitting away in my greenhouse, ranged in egg trays, three purple eyes standing to the school hymn, 'Soldiers of Christ Arise'. Inevitably, they arose in the school garden. My own revolutionary straw and comfrey potato-growing technique had its beginnings in the anarchic April planting wars of 1969. Furrows hoed, Mr Field trusted us to fetch the wheelbarrows and trays of King Edwards ourselves while he went grafting cherry trees down the orchard. We paired up; gunner in the wheelbarrow with the grenades, tank driver pushing. We fought to the last tuber.

Mr Field called it Rural Science, but it was Smallholding for Boys. In post-war Ministry of Education huts all over the countryside, the Mr Fields of England attempted to address the needs of a declining rural economy. From today's perspective, it was a radical, meaningful attempt. Pig-rearing, horticulture, wine and cheese making, practical craft-work like hurdle and besom broom making, haystack construction, tree planting, hedge-laying, garden tool repair and maintenance, the art of the compost. It was both behind and ahead of its time, falling as it did at the doomsday cusp of English rural culture, the final days of peasant heritage. We boys too were subject to the denaturing of the times. Junk food and industrialised farming was changing the landscape and the kitchen. The hop gardens were closing down as Guinness pulled out. The cider makers went into quick oblivion and the poor just stopped eating our fruit. At school-leaving we were sent to town, turned off the land, pointed wrong-wards into the plasticating end of the 20th century.

2.

Joe was an old-time gardener lost in his cups, retired from the palace gardens. We lived in paraffin-fugged bedsits in a jaded brick house with a walled garden off Eton Square, hidden round the back of Belsize Park. His compost heap was pure Swattenden, built of leaf mould in three, six feet cubes. A barley wine tenor, he sang in the stairwell, just the one song: 'I'll walk beside you down a country lane'. Later, I understood. It was a popular song to play at funerals.

Joe wasn't an obvious inspiration. Cap and dewdrop, knock-boned in a greasy suit, he spent the mornings drying teabags under the grill for the compost. The leaves he collected in sacks from the leafy lanes of Belsize Park and Swiss Cottage, pausing to whet his whistle, parking his bulge of sacks outside the pubs.

Country boys go to London at their peril. You have to suffer the losses as the gains dwindle. Joe showed me his garden daily. When we stood beside his leaf mould compost, I took it badly. The loss of nature in life leads to listless confusion, compensatory over-production of mediocre theories on existence, bad novels like a suppurating ailment. The time on your hands won't wash off and you save it up till one day you open life's cupboard and it falls out in a heap, like a load of empty gin bottles. You become easily influenced but your understanding of the world diminishes.

Authority becomes an enemy and you believe in everything, understanding nothing.

There were other Joes along the way, shabby men who cared little for the world, who acted like distress beacons from a mothballed alma mater. They filled the existential vacuums with their runner beans or wading staffs, their hand built carp rods or their comfrey and nettle extract. In floods of induction, they stripped the false clothes off my back and all those lost instincts and empathies poured from the lies London helps you tell. All self-conscious discourse on narratology with fellow liars was instantly irrelevant and quite useless. It's like getting your sight back; life wasn't fare-dodging in a metropolitan dump where the wildlife is a one-eyed homeless pigeon or a viral squirrel, and the countryside is Hampstead Heath.

From out of orbit, it's a long way back from the concrete coffin. The path home took a pilgrim's progress, a picaresque where you're outrunning technology's dog-catcher. But with sage nods from these men along the by-ways of Britain, I found an atavistic track to the hermitage, re-learning the practical ecologies of a disrupted rural education. I learnt how to become what I am, a mellow savage living in a yurt under an oak tree with a compost toilet and a rainwater tank, where the outside world is how the rain makes it, and a night out is an owl in an orchard.

After Joe, there was Wilf in mid-Wales, always clobbing round the village in his wellys, four-inch dewdrops under his nose. Gardener, walking stick, wading staff, crook maker and part-time shepherd, you'd see him walk his own two-pint jug down to The Oak at dinnertime, then back over the fields without spilling a drop. In the afternoons he fed the sheep from paper sacks of stale bread. His cottage was on the hillside, garden sloping up to a drover's track, shed beside a low stone wall, his view just clipped the tree tops and caught a band of sea when the sun lit it. His hands were like suede work-gloves and he reeked of roll-ups and whisky. But it was his shed which woke the Swattenden boy in me. A mix of shiplapped oak and besom faggot with an overhanging shingle roof, each side was clad in feather, fur wing and tails, an ossuary of bone, skull, tails and shell. Everything his cats had dragged in for the last thirty years. One day I'll have a shed like yours, I said.

JS was a tramp who opened my eyes to wild mushroom gathering. He looked like Elias Fries, the 19th-century father of mushroom classification with his skullcap and nest of white hair, author of a great 1832 Latin bestseller *Systema Mycologicum*. Both seemed more descended from *fungi* than *homo sapiens*. He was a wild man of Hertfordshire, a genuine Curiosity Shop miser with the genius's knowledge, amounting to savantism, of the tramp's circuit, where mushrooms had their place. On mushroom specifics, his lips were sealed. He was only out to make his stake, and no man was going to steal his claim on all the mushrooms of the world. He claimed to have eaten 120 species of mushroom already. I believed him, and still do, especially now I've learnt that there are 1.5 million species and only 5 per cent have been identified.

His knowledge of mushrooms went far beyond the sensible. If it wouldn't kill him he'd eat it. If it was free, he'd take it. But he hoarded his knowledge like he did his money. His motto was *find out for yourself*; so I did.

JS didn't particularly *like* mushrooms. He was lazy and found the hunt irksome. He wouldn't share his knowledge, and he was scathing of my early failures and he mocked my ignorance. He was a curious inspiration, but he was still an inspiration, not least because he had a secret garden, hidden away where nobody could steal his peas. Here at last was nature's fence, and he sent me on my way with all I needed – two shrivelled Russian comfrey roots in a brown envelope, the secret itself, and a second-hand *Collins Gem Guide to Mushrooms and Toadstools*. Twenty years later, and seven gardens on, the descendants of those roots are the engine room of my potager, while half the year is put aside for the basket and knife, the thrill of the forage.

And last there was Harry, seventy-seven, the widower next door who grew onions and spuds between his coal shed and the sea wall on the rocky path to Dunstanburgh Castle on the Northumberland coast. We were always at sea there, our windows glazed in salt, the wind blowing our gates off. Waves bellied over the rocks fifty yards from our back doors and we'd meet in the dark, moseying out to our coal sheds in our slippers to feed our fires one shovel at a time. I'd have to shout double to be heard over the wind and into Harry's ear-drums, perforated from the shells on 'Omaha' beach. We'd shout of onions and scavenging driftwood, of the lonely men who won't go in pubs and who weep out to sea. We'd fish for lobsters and dogger crabs with our pots along inshore gullies, but it was the onion shouts by night which made me an onion grower. Harry buried the sets so deep the wind couldn't shrivel them black.

Mr Field, Joe, Wilf, JS and Harry, rural scientists of the countryside arts who pulled a Swattenden boy back to his place in life. Any lost soul of nature only has to listen to such men, downwind of instinct. There are plenty of Joes left, though I suspect all five of mine are buried deeper than the wind themselves by now.

Hush

Robin Turner

'There's no such thing as silence. What they thought was silence, because they didn't know how to listen, was full of accidental sounds.'

John Cage

Does absolute silence exist? I'm not talking about the kind of zoned-out peace and quiet we get when snatching a coffee break at work; those five precious Zen minutes away from ringing telephones and pinging emails. No, that's the 21st century's blunt, pallid impression. What I'm talking about is pure, flat silence. The total absence of sound. Pretty much impossible in the situations most of us move through on a daily basis, it's something of a Holy Grail. Sound pollution is ubiquitous like the dull orange throb of light pollution around our towns and cities. Each bleeds into every available space. And nature – given the chance – is as guilty as us of helping fill any silent voids.

Think of a languorous, woozy afternoon in high summer, whiling away stolen hours in countryside that rolls out like a Constable painting. Serenity soon cross-fades into bird-song and the rattle and click of insect industry. Even the sway of leaves in the idlest of breezes seems harshly amplified, wheat ears swishing violently while crickets keep their metronomic time signatures somewhere out of view, always just past eyesight. Or picture yourself wandering alone on the coast, far away from busy roads and barking dogs, dementedly sprinting free from their leashes. Quickly, your ears retune to the ebb and flow of the ocean. The artillery roll as pebbles shift endlessly up and down the shoreline could be distant cannon fire or the music of collapsing buildings, the world-weary drag and drop of stones as they constantly rearrange like a prehistoric penny arcade machine.

Tennyson's observation that nature was 'red in tooth and claw' speaks volumes about the carnality of the wild world, yet it's the warlike thunder that comes with it that never fails to amaze me. I once heard Chris Watson – a man whose life's work has been an aural dedication to the natural world – describe birdsong as less a pretty distraction and much more a statement of defiance sung out at daybreak by survivors to potential predators; something akin to 'C'mon, have a go if you think you're hard enough!' rendered in lyrical cheeps. A mocking declaration to baldly state, 'You didn't get me. I am still here.'

It's odd how obsessed we are with trying to promote silence in forced situations. We think putting up a few signs will conjure a mellow atmosphere, maybe even encourage concentration. The quiet carriage on an intercity train, peopled by the anti-social and the just plain relieved, all ready to pounce on anyone with an unchecked mobile or a pair of errant headphones. The school gymnasium under exam conditions, purged of the sound of wet weather play-time. In the stuffy breeze that blows between tomes in our dusty and beleaguered libraries, where speaking volumes inevitably leads to a matronly 'Shhhh!' Or – at its most forced – under police interrogation, avoiding questions. Exercising the right to silence.

Maybe living in Hackney – paradoxical home of ever-spiralling house prices and ever-more-brutal council cuts – my ears have retuned to the point that they repel silence. The vibrations of double-deckers and the wasp-like buzz of police sirens have become the all-encompassing tinnitus of daily life. The city seems to run on the bass drones of pirate stations, the tinny rasp of mobile phones on buses and the crunch of chicken bones underfoot, our unavoidable and thoroughly modern urban carpet. When I migrated to the Smoke from Wales at the turn of the '90s Hackney was full of portentous silences, the enveloping pin-drop quiet that washes over with all the ominous calm of an airlock. Never further from nature, the city was more *noir* than ever; silences of the kind punctuated by footsteps and bag snatches, breaking glass and car alarms.

And the years since? I'd begun to doubt silence. City living will do that to your head. Sure, there must be centres of Hebridean islands or deep points in Scottish valleys where the wind doesn't howl and where prey birds swoop in graceful, murderous freefall. On the whole, though, in Britain we've smoothed out so many rough corners, re-land-scaped our wild places. To me – an occasional coastal tourist and inland walker who has never strayed too far from culti-vation-by-way-of-The National Trust – peace and quiet always comes coupled with the crunch of a wood-chipped path or the harsh metallic lullaby of the ice cream van. Everywhere seems to come with a soundtrack; subliminal yet inescapable.

But then – when you're not expecting it – nature comes and interjects, changing its own rules right in front of you.

A cold, cold December. The kind where eye-boggling stats are rattled off on news programmes, where schools stay closed and the clamour to huddle up to pub fireplaces is like the rush for the proverbial last boat out of Saigon. The kind where the floorboards creak and buckle as central heating seems to surge permanently through the pipes. As people made plans for the festive season, weather systems gathered and plotted their own monumental rearrangements.

First a blanket of snow, then a carpet, before finally turn-ing to something with a shagpile of epic tottering propor-tions. Where it usually turned grey to sludge with a disinterested shrug after a few glorious hours, now it stub-bornly refused to shift. In Cardiff – my family's seasonal destination – a friend described his garden as being 'bollock deep. The whole place is like the Lion, the Witch and the fucking Wardrobe.' And with that came a dazzling white-bright silence. All sound had been razored away, bleached back to nothing. It could almost have been scripted, like the prelude to the *Dr Who* Christmas Special with the mute button stuck in position. Call it the icy flipside of climate change or posit it as an Act of God if that's your thing, but this was a Christmas sent specifically to bate the good people at Ladbrokes.

Back before it became Llan-Narnia, there would once have been garden after garden of avian scavengers. Now in this whiteout world there was no mocking, just a mute acceptance of circumstance. Here, robins, thrushes, black-birds, mistle thrushes, wrens, collared doves, tits, wagtails and wood pigeons each took turns and formed orderly queues to sombrely peck peck peck at hand-cast seed that only cleared the first few feet of snow-covered lawn. A pack of near-feral neighbouring cats was too brittle and frost-bitten to put up a fight. Mortal enemies were recast as fellow apocalypse survivors, stalking through the garden for scraps – part Richard Adams, part Cormac McCarthy. Nature's assertion of dominance had taken everyone by surprise. For us – safe and warm behind triple glazing and dry stonewalls – interaction didn't stretch to much more than slack-jawed observation and the occasional fistful of Trill thrown out of the kitchen window.

A family tradition – mine and my father's Boxing Day walk from Southerndown to Ogmore for the traditional umpteen pints around a crackling fire – had gained a new set of problems. Usually twenty brisk minutes over briar and bracken, then through the heart of a golf course dodging shanked shots, today was a stealth mission through a bleached world finally at peace with itself.

We were explorers lurching out over an entirely new geography. A booze-hungry Scott and Amundsen striking out towards the Pole, Han Solo searching desperately for a half-decent pub on Hoth, snow-bitten yet alive, we were desperate drinkers in a world where snow had deadened all sound. Our feet seemed to glide through the drifts making no impact sounds. Everywhere we looked, the animal kingdom had bowed down in deference to nature. A few dozen scraggy ewes bundled together, rooted to the floor, appeared frozen in shock as much as anything else.

There was no birdsong.

No barking.

No bleating.

No breeze to shake the trees.

No Sunday drivers, no chaotic sirens.

No lines reeling, no mountain bike wheels spinning.

No crunch of feet, no sharp breeze.

No nothing.

Silence here wasn't golden. It was a dizzying white accompanied by a hush that didn't break for miles and miles. After a while, conversation respectfully fell away. We were quickly adapting to the heaviest snowfall in years, cautiously picking through untrodden paths, surfaces re-landscaped in powdery white here on a planet reborn with the speakers unplugged.

The next day, foggy-headed after a few too many, the thaw has begun. Silence once more seemed illogical – impossible – as icicles dripped noisily, sploshing onto the paving stones. The garden spluttered back to life while natural enemies shook sense into themselves and began their evolutionary stalk; either pensive and defensive or greedy with bloodlust.

Slowly, the world blinked itself back awake, colour gradually filling the cheeks as normal life resumed.

Volume again audible.

How to Tell the Difference between ...

Frogs and Toads

In the UK there are a number of different species of frogs and toads, though of course the most regularly seen are the Common Frog and the Common Toad. Even these two species are often identified incorrectly, so I thought it might be useful to explain some simple ways to be able to distinguish between frogs and toads.

Generally speaking, the Common Frog is more likely to have a more pointed face than the Common Toad, which tends to have a rounder and blunter face. Frogs also prefer to hop while toads will generally walk, unless they are surprised and want to make a quick escape.

The skin also helps you tell the difference between the two species. The frog's skin is generally smooth and shiny-looking, whilst that of the toad is generally warty and often has a matt-effect look to it.

The toad has a poison gland behind the eye which looks like a large swelling, and this is absent in the frog.

Lastly, in the breeding season the eggs of these two species look very different. Whilst the frog lays its frogspawn in a large jelly-like mass, toadspawn is laid in long, thin strands rather than one large mass.

There are, of course, just as many similarities as there are differences. They both breed in water. They will both jump if surprised or scared. They generally eat similar prey. They will often be found away from water when out of the breeding season (though they will still like moist areas such as hiding under rocks or under thick plant cover).

Even the colours of these two species can be so variable that saying that toads are brown and frogs are green isn't entirely correct and can't really be used for identification purposes.

Eating the
Landscape

John Wright

Asking someone why they forage for food rather than buy it in the shops is like asking someone why they walk when they could drive or catch the bus. Foraging, like walking, is one of our basic modes of operation – something we were born to do – and nature has made all such pursuits pleasurable experiences for us. Queuing in the supermarket or travelling at 23 mph on the M25 are *not* natural and there is certainly no pleasure in them – nature did not know we would need to do such things. Nevertheless, some people still ask me why I will cheerfully thrash around in a prickly, fly-infested blackberry bush or wade, bewellied, through a watercress-clogged stream when I could easily buy blackberries or watercress from the market for next to nothing. Well, apart from the fact that 'next to nothing' is still more than 'nothing', it is enormously satisfying, and that basket of blackberries or bunch of watercress becomes a thing of pride to be boasted about.

Few will boast of the two punnets of blackberries they bought from the supermarket.

Of course no one who wants to live a fairly normal life will be able to forage for more than a small part of their food – there just isn't enough time, and, although the diet would be an extremely healthy one, it would be rather odd and tragically lacking in chocolate. Those trips to the shops will still be necessary, but I do not think that matters; the experience of gathering wild food, even if just occasionally, is both salutary and enlightening. One of the great pleasures of taking people on a mushroom hunt or a seashore foray is to see their eyes light up with the primal delight of the hunt; all day-to-day worries are forgotten in the single-minded pursuit of dinner. Zen and the Art of Foraging perhaps. And, apart from the sheer joy of it all, something is learnt. Food is no longer considered a commodity to be taken without thought from a shelf, but a living organism in its own ecological niche and with its own problems. And food suddenly becomes truly valued, not necessarily because it tastes better than usual, or because the forager feels, for once, that he or she really deserves it, but because often it is so very hard to obtain.

While most of us still walk – even if it is just to the car – few now forage. Certainly in the UK it is a rare pastime with a thin history. The Neolithic Briton would have obtained some sustenance from field and wood, marsh and seashore, and the peasantry through the ages have supplemented their hard-won crops with something free from nature. However, foraging has never formed the fundamental part of our culture that it has in so many European countries. Perhaps our isolated, maritime location has protected us from both war and extreme weather – constant causes of famine on the Continent and an irresistible incentive to view every last thing as a potential meal. Nowhere is this disinclination to forage for wild food more striking than with the fungi. Britons are terrified of wild fungi, believing that they can be poisoned simply by touching one. When I began collecting wild mushrooms over thirty years ago everyone thought I was quite mad. But in the rest of Europe mushroom hunting is a regular family activity, with mushrooming lore passed down the generations.

The modern British foraging movement began in the early 1970s when Richard Mabey published his justly famous book, *Food for Free*. Now, with extensive foreign travel, endless TV cookery programmes demanding wild ingredients and the encouragement of the Internet, many more are willing to leave their back door armed with basket and knife. But the old fear is still there, so where do people start? How do they avoid making their first wild meal their last? In fact most wild foods are extremely easy to find and identify: everyone knows (usually to their cost) what a stinging nettle looks like, and blackberries, crab apples, raspberries, hazelnuts and a dozen other species will be known even to those for whom grass is the stuff that grows in the gaps between paving stones. To venture further, however, you really, really need some books. I have accumulated around 100 on the identification of plants, fungi and animals, but there is no need to join me in Anorak World – just two or three will suffice.

What's on the menu?

I have a fairly broad definition of foraging – collecting anything edible that does not belong to anyone else and which can be captured without recourse to a fishing line or a gun. If we ignore such gourmet delicacies as signal crayfish and garden snails, this leaves us the flowering plants, the fungi, seaweeds and shellfish – plenty enough to satisfy the chef.

It is impossible to mention all but a few of the many hundreds of edible species found in this country, but perhaps we could go for a walk …

The flowering plants

I have my basket ready on my arm but instead of going out the front door I go out the back. My lawn has suffered from the attentions of children, over-wintering kayaks, swing-ball stands and general neglect, and amongst the weeds grass has become a minority species. Two weeds in particular thrive there.

Ground elder is a notorious, parsley-like leftover from the ancient kitchen garden. When the gardener found better plants to grow – notably parsley – he found himself in the position of the apocryphal Australian Aborigine who, having acquired a new boomerang, couldn't get rid of the old one. Ground elder persists in very many gardens and is all but ineradicable. Even experienced wild-foodies can be a little sniffy about this extremely useful plant, describing it as bitter and tough. Their mistake is to pick mature leaves, whereas only those that are very young, folded and bright yellow/green are worthwhile. These taste like the best parsley and are much more succulent. As even I mow my lawn on occasions, new growth is encouraged and ground elder is available for half the year.

Only slightly less persistent is the humble dandelion. If you have ever nibbled dandelion leaves you will know how intensely bitter they are, and a salad of them would be too much for even the hardiest of palates. However, they are a little milder in the first, fresh growth of the year and an upturned flower-pot will blanch them in a few days to an even more acceptable mildness. The flowers become super-abundant in spring, soon disappearing almost completely to be replaced by a froth of down. Apart from the most excellent dandelion wine, the flowers can make a good floral syrup by layering equal volumes of (pressed down) petals and sugar in a tall jar and leaving for twenty-four hours before pouring over some hot water and then straining. It tastes of barley-sugar and is terrific in cakes in place of plain sugar. The best crop from the dandelion, however, is the root. Dried, roasted (25 minutes, 190°C) and ground, they make a genuinely tasty coffee-like drink. No, really they do. Dandelion latte is my favourite.

Out of the house and around the corner I come to the river. This is a chalk stream abounding in trout, the occasional eel and a few signal crayfish. But, although I am allowed to fish here, I am no fisherman so these creatures will be left in peace. Much more to my taste are two constants of this stretch of river – watercress and watermint.

Watercress can cover a stream from bank to bank for 100 metres or more and can be collected by the sack-full with no appreciable effect on the population. There are, unfortunately, a couple of problems. Frequently entwined with watercress is a lookalike – fool's watercress. Happily this is not at all poisonous, it just isn't watercress. It is a member of the carrot family and tastes, unsurprisingly, of carrots. This gives a clue to the simple way of telling one from the other – taste them.

The other drawback is more serious. Liver fluke is endemic to the British Isles and an extremely common parasite of sheep and cattle. Few rivers where they pass through grazing land are free from it. Although not a natural host, humans can easily be infected and suffer serious, sometimes fatal, infestations of the liver. Fast-flowing streams lacking muddy banks and away from grazing areas are the safest, but even here I do not like eating the watercress I find raw.

While a steriliser such as Milton's Fluid will kill the parasite, by far the best way is to cook your wild watercress. Salads are off the menu, but watercress soup is most definitely on.

Towards the edge of the river, but also easily found in ditches and even along damp footpaths, is the lovely watermint. We have about a dozen native mints but this is the easiest to find and the most useful. It is distinctly pepperminty, not suited to boiled potatoes. However, in sweet dishes, such as watermint ice cream or watermint sorbet, it is glorious. The minty aroma, hairy leaves and square stem make it an easy plant to recognise.

Eastwards and under the railway bridge I come to the local allotments – one of my best hunting grounds. Now I must make it clear that my raids on the allotments are not only totally innocent affairs but a positive boon to its hornyhanded villeins – it is only their weeds that I remove. Several vegetable-plot weeds, bane of the gardener, are good to eat.

Almost any disturbed bit of soil will quickly produce a crop of sprawling, straggling chickweed. This plant is a pernicious pest so it is good news that it is also tasty. Although acceptable in a salad the flavour of freshly mown grass is not to everyone's taste so I always cook it. Boiled it can be stringy, but in a stir-fry or mixed in a spicy chick-pea batter to make a pakora it is perfect. Chickweed is easy to identify as it has a highly distinctive single line of fine hairs running down the stem.

More substantial and even better tasting is fat hen. This is a member of the goosefoot family and the kitchen-garden forerunner of another member – spinach. Like chickweed it quickly infests any neglected piece of cultivated soil and I often find myself gently remonstrating with gardeners for digging up fat hen in order to plant the inferior spinach. What, I ask them, is the point? Quite properly they tell me to mind my own business or words to that effect. Also like chickweed, it is a 'cut and come again' plant, capable of providing two or three crops from April right up until November. The young plants, picked before the long flower spikes appear, are by far the best.

My favourite wild salad vegetable is yet another weed of cultivation. Springing up on any bare patch of land, and particularly fond of permanent borders and plant pots, is the much-hated hairy bittercress. Nearly all of it finds its way onto the compost heap, but this is such a pity – the flavour is not bitter at all, just superbly peppery and nutty, just like the cress of egg sandwiches.

Beyond the allotments and leading steeply up the hill is the 'Drift', half a mile of rough, ancient drove road, bordered by dense hedges. This is where the true 'hedgerow harvest' lies. Right at the beginning is a clump of elders – a source of elderflowers in June or (not *and*!) elderberries from late August to early autumn. Elderflower Champagne and cordial making has become something of a craze, with suburban trees quickly stripped of flowers and pharmacies of citric acid. Cordial is extremely easy to make but Champagne making is a perilous enterprise, vinegary produce or exploding bottles being the chief problems. My only advice is to obtain a recipe from an Elderflower Champagne maker with good form, keep to it strictly and make sure everything is kept sterile. The very best way to use elderflowers is as a flavouring for Turkish delight in place of roses – and if you still prefer the flavour of roses then use the highly fragrant Japanese rose which has established itself in so many of our hedges.

Elderflowers famously complement a fruit found occasionally in the hedgerow (though sadly not in the Drift) – the gooseberry. This shrub hides itself amongst the hawthorn which has vaguely similar leaves, but is easy to spot early in the year as it leafs before most other hedgerow plants. Gooseberry and elderflower fool is a food of the Gods.

A common but rather disappointing shrub is the redcurrant. The Drift is full of it, the pale pink blossom adorning the hedge for fifty-metre stretches. Although these flowers make one of the best hedgerow teas, it is usually the berries that are collected. Sadly, despite the blossom's early promise, few make it to maturity and a good harvest is rare. The familiar redcurrant jelly seems a little too prosaic a recipe for such a hard-won crop, so I make a gloriously tart redcurrant table jelly, setting inside it wild strawberries or raspberries.

Along a more sheltered stretch, beneath some ash trees that have outgrown their hedgerow duties, is a lush swathe of stinging nettles. I am afraid that nothing is more likely to put people off wild food than nettle soup. There is, of course, nothing wrong with nettle soup – it is absolutely delicious – but it is often made by incompetent cooks who think that boiling up a bag full of nettles will result in a palatable soup. It will not. But a good soup is easy to make: young nettles, a good stock and a potato to provide some body are all that are needed. A word of caution: apart from the flavour, using only young nettles is essential as the mature ones (when the flower-heads appear) contain microscopic rods of calcium carbonate which can block the kidneys.

Also in this sheltered area is a group of that most famous of hedgerow favourites, wild garlic. Although the whole plant is edible, it is chiefly the aromatic leaves that are collected. Wild garlic is in the Lily family along with true garlic, and the flavour is exactly the same if a little milder. But of course we are collecting the leaves and this opens up a new area of exploration for the cook well beyond mere flavouring. The leaves can be used to make a pesto, added to a salad or wrapped around rice and meat to make dolmas.

I am a little out of breath by now but the steepest part is accomplished and the path levels and turns slightly south. Right on the track edge, stately and fragrant, appears a group of garlic mustard plants. This is not in the Lily family at all but, oddly, in the cabbage family, with tiny, white four-petalled flowers. The mild garlic flavour comes with peppery overtones and the young, heart-shaped leaves are terrific in a salad or a sandwich.

One more hedgerow plant awaits me – the most common of them all – the hawthorn. This is the quintessential hedge-row tree because it was planted by the million in the establishment of most of our hedgerows during the enclosure periods of the 18th and 19th centuries. A pity then that it is has found such small use in the kitchen. Rows of mango trees would have been considerably more welcome but we will need a bit more in the way of global warming for this cheerful possibility to become a practical one. Nevertheless there are some excellent things that can be made from the flowers and the berries. The heady blossom can, like dandelion flowers, make a good floral syrup – the strange undertone, suggestive of both corruption and passion, mercifully disappears in the making. Hawthorn is a cousin of the apple, and haws (as the berries are delightfully called) look like tiny apples, complete with a central pip and a fleshy outer layer. Unfortunately the flesh is relatively thin and haws present a challenge to the cook. By far the best way to use large quantities of haws is to engage another hedgerow fruit – the crab apple – to make a fruit leather.

Stew equal quantities of crabs and haws with a little water for half an hour. Mash to a coarse puree, then strain through a sieve and place in a clean saucepan. Heat through and dissolve some sugar to taste, spread the sweetened puree on a baking-paper-covered tray and leave in a very low oven (60°C) for a few hours until dry. The resulting 'leather' is delicious, very good for you and costs very little. I have a dream that every year, on a Sunday in late September perhaps, family groups will forgo their trip to the supermarket and instead collect several kilos of haws and crabs to make their annual supply of haw leather. We could call it Haw Sunday.

Already overburdened I leave the Drift and enter open fields. The first two are frequently ploughed and produce nothing for the forager, but soon I am on permanent pasture and in the realm of the grassland fungi.

Nearly everyone is frightened of wild fungi, and rightly so, and I am frequently asked how on earth you make sure you do not poison yourself. Old wives' tales about silver spoons and being able to peel the skin are dangerous nonsense. There is only one safe way to tell – you find out the name of your prospective dinner. For this you will certainly need at least two good field guides. Collect just a couple of specimens (more will likely be wasteful) to take home to identify, making sure to carefully dig them up as the base of the stem will often have important identification characteristics. Make a note of where they are growing – beech wood, oak wood, pasture and so on – and how they are growing – on wood, in rings, in tufts, etc.

The temptation when you get home is to flick through you books to see if you can spot a picture that 'looks a bit like' your specimen. While we all succumb to this temptation on occasions it is not the right way to do things. Put your books away for the moment and instead study your specimens. Make a note of as many characteristics as you can: is the cap scaly, smooth, sticky, fibrous, etc.? Does the fungus have gills or tubes or spines under the cap? How are they attached to the stem? Is there a ring on the stem? Is the stem crumbly, fibrous, hollow, etc.? Is the base of the stem swollen, tapered, rooting? Does it have a bag around it? What does the fungus smell like? And so on. You should be able to come up with at least thirty things you can say about your specimen and by this time you will know it very well.

One terribly important characteristic not mentioned above is spore colour. If you have no idea what you are looking at then this is the first thing to discover. Make a stem-sized hole in a piece of paper, place it over a drinking glass and sit the fungus on the paper with the stem through the hole. After a couple of hours, or, better still, overnight, you will get a spore print. The colour will range from white through various creams to yellows to browns and black. Sometimes you will find a pink spore print. In themselves they will not tell you precisely what your specimen is but they are extremely useful in narrowing down your search.

You will now be ready to open your books. Some will have a key, a questionnaire which uses elimination to arrive at a species or genus (group of closely related species) name. Or it may have photographs of typical specimens from the various genera.

Identification of the fungi is not particularly easy; you will have to work at it and put up with a certain amount of frustration, but once you have learnt what a chanterelle, a hedgehog mushroom, a cep or a horse mushroom looks like you are set for life. And you do not need to know more than a dozen species to enjoy an abundance of wild mushrooms.

While those old wives' tales are absurd there is one gener-
alisation which has some truth to it: grassland fungi tend to
be much safer than woodland fungi. Death caps, destroying
angels and deadly webcaps are denizens of the woods,
whereas the only poisonous fungi commonly found in
grassland is the yellow stainer – a field mushroom lookalike
which can cause uncomfortable gastrointestinal activity but
no more. But remember: grassland species are not necessarily safe, just safer.

The pasture beyond the Drift sports nearly every one of
the common edible grassland species. Giant puffballs, horse
mushrooms, field mushrooms, field blewits, parasols,
meadow waxcaps, scarlet waxcaps, fairy ring champignon
and, in the spring, St George's mushrooms are all there.
None of these are hard to identify and they can grow in
enormous numbers.

It is difficult to choose a favourite from the above list but
the most extraordinary must be the giant puffball. This is
best picked at about 30cm across while it is still young, firm
and pure white inside. If left it can grow to 60cm or even
more, but both texture and flavour suffer. As it matures
further it starts to sweat profusely, turns greenish then
brown and eventually becomes a dry mass of fibres holding
an astronomical number of spores. For once 'astronomical'
is an accurate simile, as a typical giant puffball will produce
several *trillion* spores. Giant puffballs are best when fried in
some way. My preferred recipe is to peel the puffball, slice
the flesh to 1cm thickness, break the slices into biscuit-size

pieces and fry in a little butter with salt on one side. Turn them over, add a little more butter, fry, then pour on some beaten egg for a terrific giant puffball omelette.

Set within the open pasture on the slope into the valley is a fifteen-acre wood, mostly of discouraging ash and hazel. Many of the best edible woodland fungi can only grow with certain trees in what is called a mycorrhizal association; ash forms the wrong sort of association and hazel is generally associated with inedible species (with one major exception – truffles!). However, there are also some oaks and a very, very overgrown beech hedge; these, along with pine and spruce, are the major trees which host edible fungi. I find three good edible species under these trees nearly every year.

Nestling in the moss below the beeches is the beautiful and delicious chanterelle. This is a slow-growing species and I will leave specimens for several weeks to gain size before I pick them. Under the oaks there are ceps – the kings of the mushroom world and a great prize. They can suffer from maggots, but as long as the maggot-to-mushroom ratio is not too high, who cares? A great favourite and common in woodlands everywhere is the hedgehog mushroom. This is the wild mushroom with everything – it is common, delicious, never has maggots, can be found in large quantities and the distinctive irregular buff cap with thousands of little spines hanging underneath means that it is impossible to confuse with anything else.

The seashore

Shrimping

My walk, a typical one available to any who venture into the countryside, is over. But there is more to be found in these islands. I live twelve miles from the coast and spend a good deal of my time foraging there. This is where the forager turns hunter. I do not think that collecting mussels from rocks or raking cockles from the mud, or even using salt to frighten razor clams from the sand, count as hunting, but shrimping and potting do.

I made my own shrimp net by copying one borrowed from a friend, but they are available readymade fairly cheaply if woodwork is not for you. The standard push-net is a double-tee about four feet wide on which a net is fixed. Although it looks like a simple scoop in fact it is more complicated than this; the bottom tee squeezes the sand as it is pushed forward, frightening the shrimps out of their hiding place and into the net.

April and May are the best months for shrimping, starting a couple of hours before low tide and finishing an hour after low water. A sandy seafloor is essential and an absence of rocks and seaweed to be desired. Shrimping seems to have gone out of fashion – it is certainly a lot of work for small gain, and cheap prawns (a different but related species) from the supermarket have satisfied our taste for small crustaceans. But shrimping is enormous fun and its neglect over the last few decades has left many beaches unshrimped and fertile ground for the newcomer. I recently took my net to a local beach only to be told by a venerable local in head-shaking mood that he had not seen shrimps there in forty years. In twenty minutes I collected over a pint.

Crab pots

If you think shrimping hard work then try putting out pots from the beach. This involves carrying crab pots over slippery rocks, sometimes for some distance, then out at least waist deep and collecting them the next day. Just getting in and out of my wetsuit is too much effort for me nowadays. Fortunately there are now lightweight folding pots to make life easier for the ageing potter. I usually put out four pots, all tied together with a leaded rope (to make it sink) at 10-metre intervals and a plastic milk bottle to act as a buoy. Baited with fishy off-cuts and placed on sand between rocks and weed, these pots can catch a variety of species depending on what is around, the size of the pots and the diameter of their entry holes. Brown crabs of legal size are rare catches but the equally tasty but much smaller velvet swimming crab is a common catch. Two or three times a year I manage to catch a legal-sized lobster and a cheer goes up every time. In May, with a large pot, I will catch spider crabs by the dozen. It may be hard work but I cannot tell you what a joy it is to look inside a pot and see something large and delicious.

Seashore plants

The harsh environment of the seashore has produced plants which protect themselves by having thick, succulent leaves. This succulence often appeals to the human palate and some great delicacies can be found. The commonest, sea beet, is found on the upper shore. The thick, dark green leaves are distinctive, with a flavour and texture similar to but better than spinach to which the plant is related. I like it steamed in a covered saucepan for a few minutes with butter and black pepper.

Sea beet is never covered by sea water but one other succulent species gets a soaking twice a day – marsh samphire. This is a denizen of muddy estuaries and a messy plant to collect. It was once despised as a vegetable but its gourmet qualities have now been recognised and it is available, nearly always cultivated and imported, at a fairly high price from some fishmongers and greengrocers. Of course picking it yourself is much cheaper and much more fun. The plant is very variable, in fact there are half a dozen species called marsh samphire, but its branching, cactus-like appearance and muddy habitat make it an easy plant to identify. Scissors are a must, otherwise you will uproot the plant (illegal, see below) and also get mud everywhere. It is the most sensitive plant I have mentioned, so do take care in collecting it – tread carefully and cut a little here and a little there.

Seaweeds

If wild mushroom hunting is seen by the British as an eccentric activity, collecting seaweed for dinner must seem insane. Everyone knows that some seaweeds are edible but only in the loosest sense of the word. The real problem with seaweeds is that few know how to use them. Gathering half a kilo of seaweed and boiling it for dinner is just not going to work. Each of the half dozen species readily obtainable around our coast needs to be treated in a special way, and if done well some true gourmet dishes can be made from this most neglected of wild foods.

Despite what I have just said there is one species that *can* be just boiled (or preferably, steamed) and that is dulse. The purple fronds can be found at low tide on any rocky shore. The colour, along with the hand-shaped ends to the fronds, makes it an easy species to recognise. Not that it matters too much – no seaweed found near the shore is poisonous. Steamed for twenty minutes and served with butter and black pepper it is not unlike cabbage, with perhaps a hint of the medicine cabinet about it from the high iodine content.

Laver is the one species commercially collected in Britain for food, being a Welsh delicacy. The fronds are gossamer thin, green/brown membranes attached to rocks or other seaweeds (depending on the precise species). It must be cooked for up to ten hours to be made palatable, by which time it will become a dark brown paste called laverbread, which can be mixed with oatmeal and fried in bacon fat for breakfast. It must be said that laverbread does not look remotely edible and the taste does take a bit of acquiring, but I can promise you it is worth a bit of perseverance.

Having a sweet tooth my favourite seaweed is carrageen. The wiry, bushy fronds are found on the sides of rocks at a good low tide and should be cut one third of the way from their holdfast. The main use for carrageen is as a setting agent for milk desserts such as panna cotta. It is something I collect whenever I can so that I can dry it for use through-out the year.

The law

'Food for Free' is the motto, but should it really be 'Food Belonging to Someone Else'? The short answer is no. There is an ancient understanding, happily enshrined in the 1968 Theft Act, that picking wild plants (foliage, fungi, fruit and flowers) for personal consumption is not theft. The Act says that even if done on private land it is still not theft, merely a further act of trespass. But do note the words 'wild' and 'personal' – if the plant is cultivated or you sell what you pick then you will be guilty of theft. Sadly seaweeds are not included in this, so carrageen hunting will take you to the dark side. Not that anyone will care.

While it only affects a few of the plants likely to be of interest to the forager, the 1981 Wildlife and Countryside Act makes it an offence to dig up any plant from any land without the permission of the landowner. This is a pointless bit of government meddling as it was a law introduced for no conceivable purpose – digging up rare plants was already an offence. So if you want some wild horseradish or those dandelions along the roadside you will need permission.

Nature reserves are, in principle, out of bounds to the forager, but the authorities generally accept that the restrained picking of common species for the table is not going to do any harm.

There are endless rules and regulations about where, what, when, how and how much one can collect down by the sea. My book *Edible Seashore* goes into the matter in some detail.

Conservation

It may be legal to pick things from the wild, but is it *ethical*? Some say that we have taken enough from nature already. Conservation is an issue very dear to my heart but I have absolutely no sympathy with this point of view. The vast majority of wild food plants are extremely common and some of them are weeds. We seldom collect the whole plant but rather just a few leaves, the flowers or the fruit. The common wild fungi are under no threat from mushroom hunters. Mushrooms are the fruiting bodies (spore produc-ers) of a much larger, cotton-wool-like organism which lives underground. Pick as many mushrooms as you like and you will not damage the organism. Though the parallel is not exact, picking mushrooms is like picking apples from a tree. Of course you will damage its ability to produce spores, but not every mushroom is destined for the mushroom basket and countless trillions will still be created. Some fungi are rare and need all the help they can get, which is why I suggested not collecting a basketful of any one species without knowing what it is. There is also a case to be made for leaving some fungi for others to see and enjoy and also so that invertebrates, many of which rely entirely on fungi for their existence, can find a home.

Repeatedly ripping seaweeds from an area will damage the ecosystem at that point, allowing the less than interesting wracks to become established, which is why cutting with scissors and picking here and there are essential seaweed-collecting practices. With shellfish good sense and simply obeying the law will ensure that you follow a sustainable path.

Ultimately conservation comes down to common sense – picking blackberries is fine but not if you trample over orchids to get to them. I know many dedicated foragers and many people who just collect a bag of elderflowers and some nettles in the spring. The one thing that they all have in common is a love of the wild. They, above all others, will always seek to protect it.

Bracken

Mathew Clayton

E very Sunday when I was a child my parents would herd my three brothers, two sisters and me into the family car, a large green army Land Rover, and drive over to my grandparents' cottage on Ditchling Common. After attending mass at the local convent, St George's, my brother Alistair and I were free to roam the great outdoors.

In the summer months this meant building camps in the patch of bracken that stood in front of my grandparents' house. Because of this I feel like I know bracken better than any other plant. I can immediately conjure up its smell, the feel of its symmetrical triangle of leaves, the strength required to uproot it, the powdery texture underneath your feet in the winter when it has turned a reddy brown. I love the way it springs up each year out of nothing. An instant jungle six-foot high. And then, just as you are thinking it is invincible, a heavy autumn shower will knock the whole lot down.

Last year I moved into my grandparents' old house. I was looking forward to playing in the bracken with my children. But in those intervening years something had happened to bracken. It had gone bad. It caused cancer. Calling it 'the fatal fern', newspapers declared: 'It's green, it's pretty, and it can kill you.'

It was also claimed 8 per cent of the UK was covered in bracken and it was expanding at an alarming rate. Soon it would take over the whole country and we would all die. And it wasn't just cancer. Bracken was also shown to provide the perfect breeding ground, not just for bluebells and snowdrops as I remembered, but for ticks that carry Lyme disease, a potentially fatal infection that is hard to diagnose. A classic moral panic.

Bracken is one of the world's oldest plants. Fossil records show that it has been around for at least 55 million years. You can find it all over the world – although bracken doesn't flower, it loves sunshine and mild climates. It spreads via a network of underground rhizomes that make it hard to eradicate. In folklore it was believed that if you cut bracken on the Midsummer Eve it would render you invisible, and in Scotland the Brown Man of the Muirs, a mythical dwarf who protected the animals of the borders, was said to dress in withered red bracken.

In the UK it is harvested to turn into compost, while in Japan and South America the emerging fronds – wonderfully known as fiddleheads – which taste a little like asparagus, are eaten in salads. But when these delicious morsels were fed to mice over a sustained period they all developed cancer. This is because bracken contains a carcinogenic compound called ptaquiloside. And whilst we don't eat bracken in the UK, it can work its way into the food chain. Ptaquiloside dissolves easily in water and can get washed out of the bracken and into the soil during the winter. A study by Lars Holm Rasmussen, a scientist at the Royal Veterinary and Agricultural University in Denmark, showed that there was a higher level of gastric cancer in Gwynedd, North Wales, where bracken dominates part of the country-side. Ptaquiloside can also be transferred to milk when cows eat bracken. Although it is believed that the risk in the UK is small because it is unlikely one group of cows will exclusively eat the plant, some people also believe that the bracken spores released at the height of the summer can cause cancer, if inhaled in sufficient number.

And because of all this, as I lead my children through the bracken this summer it will no longer be with the innocent pleasure I greeted this patch of earth as a child. But for me that is the real wonder of nature. That it can be beautiful, seductive, very, very old and also surprisingly deadly.

Winter Pike Fishing

John Andrews

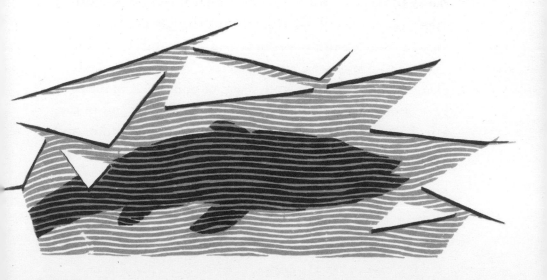

You may fish for pike in seasons other than the winter but it is to the winter that the pike belongs, for winter becomes the pike like no other season. It is a time of darkness and stillness, the deadbeat of the year, a time when clocks stop, dust settles, breath shortens and the hungry fox barks in the wood. For the pike is unlike any other freshwater fish. He is fin and scale enough but he is as much part beast and part myth as any phantom, and lurks in the shadows and nightmares of the angler's mind. He is there just as you fall asleep and he is there just as you awake. He is as much a fish out of water as he is of it. Frequently likened to a monster, writing in *The Accomplisht Lady's Delight* (1685) Hannah Wolley said of him: 'Pike: in the first year Shotterel, in 2nd Pickerel, in the 3rd Pike and in the 4th, Luce,' whilst Bickerdyke said of them, 'Pike, are anything but vegetarians,' and Franck summed things up: 'He murders all he meets.'

If you walk the margins after the first frost has cleared the water of the last of the summer algae you will meet this murderer, like a Magwitch unchained upon the marsh. The pike is outlaw, thief, loner, cold-blooded killer. You will tackle up for him like a vigilante gone crazy on a cocktail of desperate prayers and strong liquor, and in your pocket will be Henderson's elasticum wire, gimp, cruelly barbed treble hooks of steel sharpened upon an oiled stone, drilled bullets, lucky teeth, tested swivels, Gazette Bungs painted red, lines of a high breaking strain, rods that will not break, reels with greased ratchets, stout pliers and forceps stolen from a surgeon's trolley, an outsize net big enough for you to step in, a sack big enough in which to spend the night and a tape to measure your convict should you catch him. You may search for him at the bottom of brick pits, in urban bomb holes, in outlying farm ponds, along chill fen dykes, during picnics by hanging rocks, in reflecting millpools, amid lonely woods, in the poetry of Ted Hughes and in the lies of poachers, on rushing Thames weirs, by spooky backwaters, along tributaries not marked on any map, upon flooded fields, lying in deep runs, where you may find him, fins a-quiver in quiet slacks, eyes cold amid root-filled caves, formed in legions along military canals, under mats of rubbish in neglected municipal lakes, on lost glacial tarns, and nailed to the wall like the last piece of garlic in a Christian world, high in a glass case above the fire and every time without fail in the imagination of the terror-stricken and of those gone mad.

There are places known to be close to the centre of your civilisation where you may also fish for him should you have the nerve. Places such as The Serpentine in Royal Hyde Park, of which Princess Lieven wrote in 1820, 'Good society no longer goes there except to drown itself.' You may fish in waters dug by early 19th-century men without morals such as the Royal Military Canal that runs from Shorncliffe in Kent for twenty-eight miles to Cliff End in East Sussex. Twenty-two and a half miles of its length were dug by hand as a defence against feared Napoleonic invasion and such was its importance that the newspapers of the time reported on every aspect of its construction: 'last week the wife of one of the men employed in the cutting of the canal at Shorncliffe was conducted by her husband to the market place at Hythe with a halter around her neck and tied to a post whence she was purchased for sixpence'.

You may catch one in the Vale of Health upon Hampstead Heath, where in 1777 the Hampstead Water Company enlarged the pond and drained the marshy ground. You may look for the ghost of a pike along Nelson Street in the East End where once stood Wellington Water, a large inland sea that Salter wrote of in *The Angler's Guide* (1815), 'situated between Bethnal Green Road and the Hackney Road [and is] well stocked with fish, kept for the angler's diversion, at a half a guinea per annum subscription'. A water that was rumoured to harbour pike bigger than the legendary Dowdeswell fish, '60lb, length of head 11 inches, between the eyes 3½ inches, girth around the shoulders 2 feet'. If you go north you may fish for pike at a place mentioned by Eric Marshall-Hardy writing in *Coarse Fish* (1942), 'about two miles south of Darlington are two ponds of small diameter but great depth, of unknown origin and known locally as Hell's Kettles. Pike abound to the exclusion of all other fishes except sticklebacks in these peculiar pits and in such numbers that I have myself caught over thirty in less than an hour.' Or you may wish to fish for pike on an estate lake such as the one at Blenheim Palace where punts are hired for the purpose. In its 250 acres you may see a descendant of the fish that Sir Edward Hutchings of Oxford caught sight of in 1814 as it pursued and seized 'another pike of considerable size'. Hutchings's boatman drove the assailant away with his 'boat-pole' only for it to sink out of view.

Knowing what you know now you may not wish to fish alone and many are advised to fish with a companion. Who better than a boatman or a guide, one who knows the haunts and habits of your quarry better than any, and who 'carries impedimenta and luncheon to the river, relieving his client of every item of labour'? Once upon a time if you were to fish the River Thames you could have fished with J. Wilder from the Kings Arms at Cookham or S. Wilder from the Orkney Arms in Maidenhead. With the Upjohn Brothers at the Cricketers in Chertsey, or the Kemp Brothers at The Oak in Teddington or even J. Brain Junior at Richmond. Marston, the late editor of the *Fishing Gazette*, said of Brain Junior, 'I have fished with him and know he works hard. He knows the bream and barbel holes and also the BEST places for pike fishing in summer time as well as in winter.' If a Thames Professional is beyond your pocket, you could try the companionship of dogs, frowned upon by some modern anglers but blessed in the November of 1916 by W.M. Gallichan who used his as beaters:

> If the water is shallow and there is much boating, depend upon it that most of the pike, especially the older and heavier ones, will spend the greater part of daylight amongst the reeds. There may be plenty of pike in the lake but not one to be seen in open water. The only remedy is to drive the pike from their retreat about an hour before beginning to fish. If the water is sufficiently shallow and the bottom fairly firm, you can put on wading stockings, go into the withered reed beds and poke about with a pole. A couple of good water spaniels are very useful for this kind of beating.

The choice of bait is very much yours, whichever will tempt your devil. Some swear by the fish of the sea, sprat, mackerel, herring; some by those of the ditch and estuary, eel or lamprey; and some by those that the pike eat every day, the small roach or gudgeon, perch or bleak. One of the largest pike ever caught, weighing 70lb and landed by John Merry, the gamekeeper to Lord Kenmure at the end of the 18th century, was landed using a peacock feather, and hungry fish have been known to swallow pocket watches. Gallichan, the

man who treated pike fishing like a fox hunt, caught pike on
the River Loddon using neither:

> I once fished for pike through a long cold day, using gudg-
> eon as live-bait. About twilight I discovered that two of the
> baits in the can were small barbel. I affixed one of these to
> the paternoster, and immediately had a run and gaffed my
> fish. I put on the remaining barbel and took a second pike
> from the same swim almost at once.

The truth is that when pike are feeding they will feed on any
offering put before them. You should not have recourse to a
barbel live-bait or to kiss goodbye to your Georgian time-
piece. They are scavengers after all. Only when they are not
so hungry do you have to experiment with different baits.

Just as there are many different baits with which to fish
for pike in winter there are also many different types of day
on which to fish. You may catch your pike in all weathers
but a settled period of weather is most conducive. The still-
water should be free of ice and the river running high but
not too hard. Like most phantoms the pike will have a taste
for food an hour either side of dusk or dawn when the light
starts to fade and the crows get restless in the trees, unless
the cold has made the ground like iron, in which case you
need to fish within earshot of a church clock as it strikes
noon. The day will be at its warmest then and perhaps the
pike will feed. And if they do not you can hasten off the
water, light a candle in your church for better weather and

retire to the nearest public house. In such weather you will not tempt him. Severe cold puts them down. Thick fog, muggy cloud, a light breeze, a cloying drizzle, all are good. Avoid the day of the gales and the nights of the moon. Dress warmly for you will do a lot of waiting, and the quieter you can be the less you will spook your quarry. As the light goes he may be less than a yard from where you stand.

When you have caught your pike, treat him as you would have done had you gone rabbiting in the woods and caught Rasputin, with a solemn awe and with the utmost of respect. Kneel down. You must let the pike recover briefly in the sack; unhook him by turning him upon his back and lying him on his back between your knees. Slide the forefinger of your left hand under the skin of his lower jaw and cock the jaw open. Should you have struck quickly upon the first take or run of your bait then amid the cathedral of teeth should be your hooks, possibly along with one or two lost by others. Take them out swiftly but carefully with forceps, cover the fish's head with a wet towel, slip him into a sack and lower him into the water to recover. At the first kick he is ready to go back. Slip the sack slowly off the head, hold the fish by the root of the tail and wait for his gills to open up. Then watch as the pike goes back through the looking glass.

Treat the pike gently and with the utmost care. Do not be tempted to weigh him unless all is at hand or you will kill your fish for certain and be left with a body on your hands and a pike on your conscience, just as Jim White had when he landed and killed the largest pike to be caught at Frensham Great Ponds in 1939, a fish that could have broken the British Record had it been left to grow out its days: 'I caught it on a 1lb perch livebait. I decided to take it to the butchers in Beaconhill and see if he could weigh it but the scales didn't go anywhere near high enough. I went onto a bulk potato warehouse in Haslemere and they weighed it.' Do not under any circumstances, other than terminally deep hooking or having landed a fish that is obviously sick, kill your prey. J. March, writing in *The Jolly Angler* (1833), would tell you different – 'This is a firm eating fish during the winter, and may be roasted or baked with a pudding in his belly' – but any jolliness will leave you as soon as you put the first forkful to your mouth. The pike is as sacred to our English waters as a cow is to the streets of Delhi. A prehistoric relic. Alive in the 21st century as much as *The Jolly Angler* is dead. If you are an angler, stalk the pike, catch him, return him and live with yourself contentedly.

For all his reputation the pike is the most delicate of all the freshwater fishes, just as Rasputin was but a man. Do not drop him on the bank, do not be tempted to curse him or to kiss him, always use a net and never be tempted to cut the line with the hooks still in him. Nurse the fish if he has come up too quickly and goes belly up. Hold him steady in the shallows and stroke his belly to get the air out of his swim bladder. If you put back a pike in a poor state he will come back to haunt you and you will sit terrorised with the mad ones in the corner, being pitied and laughed at. A wet towel or sack over a pike's head will always calm him. You will see the fins relax. Give him a bed of leaves, grass or better. Once caught this devil of a fish will become Emperor. There is nothing grander than a winter pike in his mottled splendour. You want to watch him swim away.

And if the thought of catching your first winter pike is too much for you to bear, fear not. It does not make you a coward. Be content to live with the myth. Arthur Ransome, better known as the author of *Swallows and Amazons* but happiest perhaps as the angling correspondent for the *Manchester Guardian*, wrote in praise of the uncaught fish in *Rod and Line* (1929),

> When I hear of a great pike captured where no one expected him I feel that he is a wasted fish. Better far that twenty men should fail to catch him, so that he should glorify the river for us all. The fish should have been hooked and lost a time or two, should have been watched, cruising like a submarine, should have been seen chasing pound roach as if they were minnows.

An uncaught pike is the point at which the myth is born. According to our friend J. March in his 1842 edition of *The Jolly Angler*, a Mr Baxter, Under-Park Keeper of Hyde Park in the 18th and early 19th centuries, stocked The Serpentine with '72 brace of jack' in the 1820s, 'but although he continually lay night lines and live bait trimmers for eels he never caught but one pike. There are plenty in the water, and huge.' That The Serpentine could harbour giants is not in dispute. Only as short a time ago as the 1950s a perch of 9lb was found washed up by a successor to Mr Baxter. A small predator in comparison to the pike, but still twice the size of any known perch to be regularly caught in these isles.

You may fish for pike in seasons other than winter but it is to winter that he belongs. The pike is the keeper of the winter, possibly one of the last great mythical creatures of the English countryside. As symbolic of the season as the Green Man is of the renewal and rebirth of spring. By all means go pike fishing in the winter, carry your bucket of bait in one hand, your rods and tackle in the other and the history of the fish all about you. Be wary of all of the legends and be happy in the knowledge that as your bright red Gazette float sits innocently by the reeds the pike may catch you long before you will catch him.

The Lazy Naturalist

Nick Small

Yomping across Yorkshire's moors, canoeing through the fens of Norfolk or clambering over the volcanic rocks of the North Cornwall coast are all marvellous ways of enjoying our native natural treasures at first hand. However, unless you happen to live with these wild wonders right on your doorstep, the experience is going to require serious commitment in terms of time, effort and expense, not to mention that most undesirable 21st-century monument, a carbon footprint.

Fear not, though, if you are an idle tightwad (be honest, there's a bit of that in all of us), there is another way: the Lazy Naturalist way. If trekking off into the wilderness is a tiresome and expensive chore, just bring the wilderness right into your own backyard. It's really very easy indeed. Nature desperately wants to be there; all you need to do is invite her in. Once Nature has taken up residence, you are free to indulge in the indolent practice of staring out of the window or, on summer days, kicking back on a lounger, G&T in one hand and some compact binoculars in the other, revelling in the display of bugs, birds and beasties lured by your herbaceous bounty.

The average British garden is a terrible affront to wildlife. Take its primary constituent, for example: the perfect lawn. Unless you count replacing it with decking, it's hard to imagine a more sterile and inhospitable environment. Mowing, edging, fertilising, weed-killing, moss-raking: that's a lot of time, effort and money to waste making a uniformly green and largely lifeless mat. So, be smart the Lazy Naturalist way and say: 'Sod all that.' Perfection is dull. Don't mow, just let the grass grow. Simply allow a fairly large, irregularly shaped patch of lawn to bolt completely to seed. The dancing heads of the flowering grasses catching the summer sunlight will be reward enough, but there's a free bonus for the Lazy Naturalist: insect life. All manner of bugs and butterflies like nothing more than to bugger about in the long grass, and they, Lazy Naturalist, are your best friend. Not only are they fascinating to watch in their own right, but they are also the bait which will lure larger wildlife to your private wilderness. Once this new gourmet restaurant is established a clientele of frogs, birds, dragonflies and hedgehogs will visit to chow down, secure in the safe cover of the thick jungle your bone idleness has provided for them. It won't be long before the wildflowers (aka weeds) make a comeback too. When they aren't being poisoned or decapitated on a fortnightly basis, most of them

(Yarrow, Self-heal, Clover, etc.) are, not surprisingly, keen as mustard to flourish. As well as adding textural and chromatic prettiness to your grassland, they are a great source of nectar for your burgeoning insect population.

The more of the lawn you give over, the more you'll be rewarded, although sometimes marital harmony and the kids' football requirements might necessitate compromise. The Lazy Naturalist solution is to mow less. Yes, keep an area of 'normal' lawn, but don't give it the first mow until the daisies and the dandelions have flowered, and then mow as infrequently as you can get away with. Your meadow may be large enough to mow narrow meandering paths through it, which children love, and which you can point to as evidence of 'design'. If you are still accused of being workshy with the mower, simply invite your loved ones to sit amongst the fairy rings making Daisy chains in the spring sunshine; play 'who likes butter' with a Buttercup and smugly point out that none of this would be possible if you'd brutally cut down the poor defenceless little flowers a few weeks earlier.

This brings me to another of our gardening follies: weeding. We wouldn't dream of yanking the architecturally splendid and florally munificent Spear Thistle from its home on a river bank, yet as soon as one appears amongst the bedding plants it is (in the freakish world of the normal gardener) uprooted and hurled amongst the potato peelings in the compost bin. This is insane. Don't run the gauntlet of the vicious spines or risk lower back injury. Structurally it's an impressive plant, as are most of the thistles, rich in nectar and with seeds that twittering birds are fond of pulling apart. Let it grow to its full splendour, and just see how many living things depend upon it through its phases of bud, purple flower and downy seed. It's win–win, the Lazy Naturalist way.

Take the Dandelion, for instance. It's a work of genius: a stunning golden flower, beloved of bees and other insects as an early source of nectar; and a riot of colour when much of the garden is still recovering from its winter slumber. If that wasn't enough, it produces a seed head that is a wonder of geometry as well as being one of the cleverest means of propagation on planet Earth. The Dandelion is a plant that invites you to play games, blowing at its seed to be carried on the four winds under delicate feathery parachutes to settle in pastures new. You may risk the wrath of your neighbours by encouraging this practice amongst your offspring and their chums, but it's a risk worth taking. The display gets better every year. Dandelion roots can be dried, ground and roast like coffee; its young leaves can be used in salad … and are a superb free pet food for hamsters, rabbits and lizards. Add to that the folklore of a milky sap that makes your pals wet the bed and, of course, the fact that Dandelion and Burdock (another magnificent weed) are the key flavours of the finest British pop ever invented, then it really does make you wonder why people are so hell bent on banishing them from their garden, as though they are some marauding invader or hideous virus. If this was a rare plant from some barely accessible Himalayan valley it would be a highly prized and priced garden centre 'must have'. But it's not. Thanks to the brilliant efficacy of its propagation, it's as common as muck. In the case of this wonderful plant, familiarity really has bred contempt. To the Lazy Naturalist, though, the Dandelion is a heroic stalwart of the backyard wilderness. Leave the anguish and futile battle against this iconic plant to others less shrewd than yourself, and bask in the warm glow of its sunny disposition.

There are many other so-called weeds to embrace which are quite likely to show up in your finely crafted wilderness. Nettles are excellent friends of the Lazy Naturalist. Insects love them, and they are a valuable food source for butterflies like Red Admiral, Peacock, Small Tortoiseshell and Comma. I can hear anguished cries of 'Oooh, but the children!' Gadzooks, if we mitigate all the dangers for our kids, how on earth are they supposed to develop their own risk management skills, or discover the healing properties of the Dock? Stings, scratches and bumps from the occasional tumble out of a tree are essential elements of a healthy childhood. So, encourage the nettle, the dock and prickly brambles if you are lucky enough to have them. If you're not, they will arrive in time, if you are lazy enough.

Goose Grass is another for the kids. Brilliant sticky stuff … and they can amaze their friends by nibbling on the new shoots (once they have had all the appropriate parental guidance, of course). Then there are other edible weeds like

Garlic Mustard, which is great in salads and another one beloved of butterflies (the delicate Orange Tip). There's Sorel, which has a canny habit of invading lawns, and whose flowering spikes should hopefully add some rusty hues to your waving summer meadow. Young Sorrel leaves have a fantastic lemon sherbet taste. Try offering one up to a friend and watch their initial suspicion turn to pleasant surprise when the tang hits the back of their tongue.

Without a doubt, not weeding is a crucial plank of the Lazy Naturalist way. Get yourself a wild flower book and just wait to see what turns up. Those unidentified seedlings nestling in the spring soil often turn into quite surprising grown-ups.

The OCD-afflicted sibling of Weeding is Tidying Up. British suburbia has been blitzed by an army of garden Nazis, obsessively seeking purity and perfection. It is an important element of the Lazy Naturalist philosophy to stand opposed to this tyranny of order. Neatness is our enemy: chaos, mess and tangled anarchy are our best friends.

Take autumn leaves. By all means brush them off the path, or rake them from what's left of your lawn, but, instead of wasting time, effort and money taking them to the tip or burning them, just deposit them under some shrubs, or even just find a corner to pile them up. Inevitably, an army of ground beetles, woodlice, worms, centipedes and other macro beasties will descend upon them, rendering them into nutritious pulp. You will of course know by now that hedgehogs, frogs, dunnocks and other assorted predators will soon enough arrive to take advantage of this concentrated supply of creepy-crawly grub.

The same philosophy applies to logs, branches, rocks and stones. Discreetly placed (behind bushes, in dark corners) piles of junk are very desirable to the Lazy Naturalist. For instance, an old upturned earthenware plant pot stuffed with a bit of dry grass is just debris to the untrained eye, but to a bumble bee it is a luxurious des res. If you want the wildlife to come to you, it's advisable to provide accommodation. The nooks and crannies amongst your rocks, rubble and decaying logs are just the kind of shelter wildlife is looking for. It is your mission to be messy … and if anyone protests, you can point out that you are in fact saving the planet.

Of course, if your junk is much too unsightly for your partner's taste, then you need a strategy. In this instance, enlist the help of another of the Lazy Naturalist's important allies: Ivy.

Ivy is another plant that gets a bad rep, largely because it is so successful when it gets going. The Lazy Naturalist understands that all the bunkum about it destroying masonry or dragging fences down is simply propaganda, disseminated by order-loving psychos. Ivy will quickly disguise not just your piles of rubble and assorted junk, but will also ramble around covering boring bare earth, crawling up fences and garage walls, eventually turning dull browns and greys to a luscious glossy green. The benefits of allowing Ivy to run rampant are many. Say goodbye to creosoting fences, but say hello to all the moths and lacewings that will hide amongst the evergreen leaves. Say hello to the black-birds, thrushes and sparrows that love to nest in the midst of the thick tangled stems, feeding through the winter on the plentiful fruits. Say hello to all the insects that feast vora-ciously on the sweet autumn flowers, when the rest of the garden has shut down for its winter kip. Once you have some of the common-or-garden Ivy established, you can spread cuttings around as liberally as you like. It's cheap and largely maintenance free. There are fancy varieties, too, if splashes of yellow will appease disgruntled spouses.

Whilst the accomplished Lazy Naturalist will normally avoid expending effort (and money), there are times when an initial investment is well rewarded with an enhanced nature-watching experience in the long term. The whole idea after all is to get wildlife to do all the travelling. This can be encouraged in a few ways. Clever planting is one, and that's where we 'go native' if we can, which is a key Lazy Naturalist mantra.

Trees, for instance, are vital in a couple of ways. If your garden or yard is surrounded by a fence or wall, then it's not just keeping the prying eyes of the nosy neighbours out, but the eyes of our target birdlife too. Trees protruding above the boundary of your plot are signals to passing trade that your garden might be worth investigating. They might want to come and sit in the tree to check out the lie of the land below before they are convinced it's a safe place to go.

It's not so much the size that matters, either, those with smaller gardens will be glad to know. A small native tree such as a Birch, Goat Willow or Rowan is far more valuable than a huge Sycamore. Sycamore, an alien species, will play host to very few different invertebrates (though greenfly certainly find them to their liking), whereas Birch will be home to hundreds. The added benefit of Silver Birch is that it can grow tall without casting dense shadow, it's hardy and it's pretty all year round. Elder is another. Beautiful sweet blossoms which make delicious cordial, followed by berries that birds adore. In fact, look what grows in a British hedgerow and, if you can get them, plant similar trees and shrubs. Because they have been part of our environment for thousands of years, it's not just the wildlife that has learnt to exploit their bounty. From Crab Apples to Sloes (Blackthorn) to Hawthorn, almost all have found their way into tradition and folklore as foods or remedies of some kind.

A similar logic applies to planting flowers. If you find that a visit to the garden centre is unavoidable, try to look out for plants that are as close to our native varieties as possible. There's no finer Geranium than our glorious Meadow Cranesbill. You can't beat the scent of an old-fashioned cottage garden Honeysuckle, and the berries will go down a treat with your visitors too. From herbs to heathers, primrose to pansy, violet to valerian … try to get the same variety that you'd run into on a countryside ramble. Shrubs that bear berries are normally a hit with the birds, as are Witch and Corkscrew Hazels. Vulgarity might be frowned upon elsewhere, but to the Lazy Naturalist the word 'vulgaris' in Latin plant names is usually a very good sign.

Try to plant things that belong in your environment. If you're miles from the sea, don't bother with Sea Holly. If you're near peat moorland, heathers are probably a good bet. It's pretty obvious stuff, and there's plenty of wild gardening advice on the Internet and in books. Given that the Lazy Naturalist ethos is to eschew rules and regulations, though, just do it the way that suits you best.

Probably the most important thing you can do to enhance your Lazy Naturalist experience is to create a wildlife pond. Now, I know what you're thinking: this sounds suspiciously as though physical exertion is involved. Well yes, the investment is potentially quite a strenuous one, initially at least, but the 'interest' you'll be repaid will most definitely make it worth the while. Even if you have the tiniest backyard, a half barrel of water, a dwarf lily and some reeds is better than nothing, but if you are going to do it properly, just remember to dig it deep in the middle, and have shallow edges. Introduce native Flag Iris, some common Reed, Marsh Marigold and some other native marginals and you will be amazed by how quickly it becomes the focal point for all kinds of wildlife activity. Frogs and, if you are very lucky, Newts will visit to breed, birds will drink and wash, insects will lay eggs, other insects will hunt those insects and your small mammals might even put in a surprise appearance when you least expect it. If you can pile rocks and logs to make hiding places close to the edges, so much the better. Add some movement with a pump and a trickle if you want to introduce fish (who doesn't?), and remember, where oxygenating plants are concerned, native is best. If you allow a tangled mess of Grass, Reed, Iris, Creeping Jenny, Lady's Smock (another for the Orange Tips), Speedwell and whatever else you fancy to run riot around the margins, the pond will very soon look as though it is a natural feature that has been in situ for decades. To milk your exertions to the maximum, put a bench or small table and chair alongside your miniature lake, so that you can rest your lazy behind on the balmy summer days, nurse a glass of chilled Chablis or Elderflower cordial and watch as the assorted wildlife puts on a private show to thank you for your efforts.

So, as you will have gathered, the key to getting wild creatures into your garden is to give them something in return: shelter and food. Because we're not just lazy, but Lazy Naturalists, we armchair Attenboroughs want to obviate the need to travel by luring as much wildlife in as possible. Although it seems counter-intuitive, investing in a good feeding strategy is definitely the way to go.

For the birds, it's easy these days. Almost every local supermarket has a range of feeders, seeds, suets and peanuts. Just put on a good spread and, as sure as eggs is eggs, our feathered friends will flock to us. Peanuts in hanging feeders for Tits and Greenfinches; mealworm and mixed insect crumble for Robins and Dunnocks; and if you put out niger seeds, hitherto invisible Goldfinches and Siskins will dally for long periods, pecking at the finicky husks, adding vibrant colour and twittering of an old-fashioned sort to your garden. Add to that the usual scattering of bread and seed on the lawn or on a well-placed bird table and you should have most of your bases covered. Do remember that you are lazy, though, so choice of location is vital. Ideally you want your banquet to be close enough to your window seat for you to enjoy the view, without being so close that you scare the birds off.

To the Lazy Naturalist, all wildlife is welcome. There is no room for snobbery or squeamishness. Pigeons, Magpies and Starlings in particular seem to be on the rough end of some bad press and, for some reason, appear to be resented by people who like to feed the birds. Why? Because they eat all the food? How perverse! Starlings are the Dandelions of the bird world. Take a close look at the iridescent plumage shimmering on the dullest of days, or listen to the vocal mastery as a lone bird will sit on your chimney pot, running through an endless repertoire of warbles and whistles, uncannily mimicking a huge variety of other species, some of which are probably just figments of its fanciful imagination. If you are fortunate enough to live near a roost, you might even get to witness aerial displays of flocking Starlings that would put a Disney animator to shame. It's possible that you will hear your other half, or your tidy neighbour, complaining that the food is attracting vermin: seagulls or even worse, mice. If so, excellent work, well done.

Another of these so-called vermin is the Grey Squirrel. Yes, he's an invader, but it's not his fault that he's in the wrong place. And when the bins have been rifled through in the middle of the night by the local Fox, pat yourself on the back that you have brought wildlife onto your plot without making any effort whatsoever. Try leaving a bowl of dog food out somewhere where you can see it from inside the house. If you can rig up some sort of red light, it will help you (and the kids) observe without disturbing any visitors. OK, so it might be snaffled by next door's pooch (or worse still, moggy ... more of which later) but, if you are lucky, a hedgehog, fox or even badger may come sniffing around. Who needs Kate Humble anyway?

I've just mentioned cats. If you are the owner of a cat, or you have cat-loving tendencies, then I have bad news. Cats are the enemy. The lovable moggy of the hearth rug is on a mission to seek and destroy the birds and small mammals you've carefully lured into your little wilderness the second it leaves your house. It is a lean mean killing machine, and even if you have stuffed it to its fluffy gills with kittykat, it will just kill anyway, purely for fun and sadistic gratification. If you don't have cats, do what you can to deter them. If you are a cat owner, do us all a favour and put a big bell on its collar, have all its teeth replaced with fuzzy felt or whatever you feel you can do to mitigate its destructive prowess. On behalf of all Lazy Naturalists, I thank you in advance.

So, there you have it. A year or two of measured abstinence from the labours of mowing, weeding and tidying, allied to some judicious encouragement of your garden allies, and you should have all the nature you need to watch, to investigate, to examine and to marvel at, with the minimum of tiresome exertion. You will find creative reward as you play the role of a benevolent God in your own tiny private universe. The little decisions you take can make an enormous difference to the visible, and invisible, inhabitants of your world.

If you have a fondness for anoraks, train-spotting and list-making, then you are almost certainly male, so will find great reward in keeping a running audit of the wildlife in your domain. As the list of different residents and visitors grows over the years, you will glow warmly, quietly acknowledging to yourself that the Speckled Wood on the Field Scabious would not be there without you. When you find your first Newt, basking in the pondweed, you'll be thrilled as you furtively scribble an entry into your notebook (furtively, because your wife has already made it clear that she thinks you are weird, bordering autistic).

If you are not a man, though, you will simply enjoy the loveliness that is out there: the ever-changing palette of colour, the soap opera of twittering, humming, buzzing, all-singing all-dancing Life. For it will be lovely, and those that denigrated your ambitious vision as nothing more than evidence of your tendency towards the workshy and the scruffy will, I guarantee, be cooing with approval once it all matures. This is because, when we stop interfering, nature can take our debris, our rubble and our scorched earth and imbue it anew with vivacious beauty. It's what she does, when we let her.

Cycling Round the British Coast

Nick Hand

W hat is it like to set out from your front gate with your bicycle towards the coast and, once there, head clockwise (or anti-clockwise if you prefer) for around 4,600 miles and three months until you get back to where you started?

After a little bit of digging around on the Internet – and the purchase of a nice shiny bike made for the job – that's exactly what I did. Then I added a kind of lap of honour around the Irish coast.

I'm not a full-on lycra, weekend cyclist. Far from it actually. And I truly believe anyone can do this. In fact, I think everyone should do it. It would be one of the best things you could ever do. It will be brilliant, even though it's a bit weird when you get back.

Here's a few quick tips to get you started:

- First off, you have to ride from your front door and return to the same front door.
- You should do some planning, but not too much.
- You will need a tent and a sleeping bag.
- You need to decide whether to go either clockwise or anti-clockwise. I went clockwise, because you're always a little nearer the sea.
- Go when the days are long.
- Don't take too much stuff.
- Don't take a camera crew with you.

And a slightly longer thought:

It's best to go on your own. If you go with someone else, it will be like going to a party with someone and chatting to them most of the time. In other words, you'll miss a lot of interesting stuff. Also, if you're on your own, you can go fast or you can go slow, and you can stop when you like. Basically, you don't have to check with the other person.

Having said that, I can recommend riding with friends for a stretch when you get the chance, especially when there is a pub at the end of it.

It's not too scary a thing being on your own for so long. It's not like you're going to be attacked by wolves. Although you might get the odd rock lobbed at you by a disgruntled youth (that's what they do).

I think different people would have different reasons for heading off on a 5,000-mile bicycle journey. For me, it was a mixture of:

'Blimey, I've no idea what I'm good at, what I'm capable of, but it would be nice to find out.'

Along with:

'It would be nice to see a bit more of my country, there are loads of bits I've never seen.'

And a bit of:

'I really like being on my bike.'

It wasn't difficult to put those things together and end up on my bike heading across the Severn Bridge towards Wales.

I had read a few books of journeys that inspired me. One of these was Laurie Lee's *As I Walked Out One Midsummer Morning*. It's about the journey from his Cotswold home across Spain just before the outbreak of the Spanish Civil War. I really liked how he told the story through the people that he met along the way. So this was something I wanted to do myself. I came up with the idea of making little sound-slides: recording conversations with people I met. I took out my voice to just leave them telling their story and illustrated the conversation with photographs of them, their homes, their workshops or their gardens. I aimed to seek out makers or artisans – people who make their living from a specific skill and spend their time doing something they are really passionate about. I liked the word 'artisan', because it could be craftsmen and women but could also be musicians, actors, fishermen or a cyclist.

Just to make it a bit more of a challenge, I wanted to edit and upload the stories on the road so they would have an immediacy – a bit of a rough edge but enough to tell the story of the people I met.

And so one June afternoon I set off from our house, waved off by family and friends, to wobble up the hill on my impossibly heavy bike. Weighed down by my indecision about which camera lenses to leave behind (I took the lot).

Riding a heavy bike is the cycling equivalent of driving an articulated lorry. It's a whole different experience to normal riding. You have to give up any pretence of being the fastest kid on the block and accept that a steady slow speed is as good as it gets (apart from rolling down hills). The weekend lycra kids will whizz by in a blur.

My first night's stop was in Cardiff where a couple of friends, Patrick and Jess, put me up. I immediately ditched all of my camera equipment apart from my trusty camera body and a 50mm fixed lens.

After Cardiff, I headed around the Gower peninsula and spent my first night under canvas. There is something very satisfying about arriving at a campsite under your own steam, unloading the panniers and making your own place to lay your head. I should mention that it was worth getting the tent with a porch big enough to drag my bike into, and a good warm sleeping bag.

I was still ditching gear at Tenby and again more with friends in Cardigan. It felt a bit like one of those Apollo missions, where some huge craft leaves Cape Canaveral but by the time it's in space it's a tiny little capsule. By this time (Pembrokeshire/Ceredigion) I was getting into some pretty beautiful countryside, getting into my riding and had made my first few soundslides as well.

I had sought out some of the off-road routes which are the most relaxing and often beautiful places (as is the one that sweeps along the coast near Swansea). I sometimes listened to a bit of music on these routes. I didn't make a habit of listening to music generally while I rode. Much later in my journey, I met up with the great Fearghal O'Nuallain (who along with Simon Evans became the first Irishmen to cycle around the world) and he told me, 'Of course, I listened to music the whole way around,' as he added (a bit harshly if you ask me), 'You're a different generation and wouldn't understand.'

One of the best things about being on a bike is that you don't miss anything and you get to see the little nooks and crannies of the country that you never normally see. I like the little bits of coast that stick out at funny angles. One such bit is Shell Island, just before the Lleyn Peninsula on the North Wales coast. I stopped at a huge rambling campsite here and walked through the dunes to admire the view of the Snowdonian mountains across the bay. Shell Island gets cut off by the tide and there is something a bit timeless about it, in a kind of Dennis Potter 'Forest of Dean' kind of way.

I haven't mentioned hills yet. Hills are interesting on a heavy bike. My hill technique is to set a pace, which is normally as slow as I can go without falling off, and carry on as long as I can. Sometimes I'm just knackered and have to stop to get my breath back. If a car passes at this point I grab my water bottle and pretend to be having a drink. Degrees of difficulty are measured by how often I have to stop. Occasionally someone will call out from their garden and ask if you are OK; frankly it's often difficult to answer, so a nod and a thumbs up will do. The number of hill stops got a little less as I got fitter and stronger, but some of those big Welsh, Cumbrian, Scottish and Cornish hills still demanded three or four 'water' stops.

The reward for the climb is the immense speed that you go downhill thanks to the weight of the bike. Sometimes, if the hills are continuous, you can use the momentum from a downhill to get all the way up the next climb with little effort.

I should mention that I was writing a blog every other day. I used Twitter as a kind of on-the-road diary. Anything that happened, I would put it on Twitter. Stuff that happened is all logged there. So, for example, if a little kid who took one look at my laden bicycle and shouted to me, as happened in Ravenscar, 'You must have a lot of books, like,' I logged it on Twitter.

Through the blog and Twitter, I started getting some welcome offers of places to stay. In North Wales I stayed with Paul Sandham. Paul said that I should definitely ride around Anglesey, which was just up the coast from his place. Having decided not to ride every little road next to the sea available to me, I decided to skip some bits and Anglesey was one that I had thought I might mosey on by.

But I heeded Paul's advice and headed over Telford's lovely suspension bridge and onto the island. I ended up riding around many islands on the trip. Islands are always surprising and have their own personality from the mainland. Anglesey was no disappointment. From a riding point of view it is a lovely flat ride with a dramatic climb as you leave (or as you start, depending on your direction). The other thing about islands is that there is often a lot of ancient stuff. Anglesey is covered with little roads and many standing stones and stone circles; a very beautiful and peaceful place.

Our friend Bea gave me strict instructions as I left their house in Colwyn Bay that I was not, under any circumstances, to talk to anyone – or for that matter to stop – in Rhyl. Local knowledge I think is always a valuable thing.

The Wirral has a lovely cycle track down the middle, much of it on a disused railway line, cutting through amazing high rocks at one point. It is also hilarious because it is wealthy footballer country, with huge gated mansions and loads of sports cars. It's like a footballers' wives theme park. In the end I was happy to escape and looked forward to my romantic vision of arriving in Liverpool on the Mersey Ferry with the sun glistening on the Liver bird. Unfortunately my timing was out and the ferry terminal was shut. I got a bit lost in Birkenhead – probably not the best place to take a wrong turn – but have got to say the locals were (dead) helpful (like). I manoeuvred my bike into a lift and onto the tube train. So the romantic moment was had travelling through a tunnel under the Mersey. Timing is a tricky thing on a bike.

Beyond Liverpool I stopped briefly to ask people in Crosby what they thought of Antony Gormley's 'Another Place'. Then on to Southport. After finding a B&B, I headed off in search of food, which was always a bit of a panic as we seem to have a food curfew in Britain after 8.30 p.m. On this occasion the Italian restaurant down the road was full. As I headed back to find Pizza Express the owner chased after me. He sent me to another Italian and told me to tell Boris 'Gino sent me' and I would be well looked after. This I did. The food, at £15 for three courses, was excellent. Later Boris leant over and whispered, 'How long you know Gino?'

I made a soundslide in Morecambe, a sort of homage to Eric Morecambe, who died 25 years ago. Then, on a little cycle path just past Workington, I met Harold, who – with his strange long fishing poles – took two hours a day feeding red squirrels. Harold was keeping the population alive; the red squirrels were thriving and have somehow avoided the battering from their scraggy grey cousins that have finished them off in most of England.

There's no getting away from it, Cumbria is hilly. I met three shocked Dutch cyclists on the road here. I suppose hills were new to them. Here, too, you get your first glimpse of Scotland over the Solway Firth. On a ride in the long summer evening north of Workington, I saw a dazzling Yellowhammer and, minutes later, a Barn Owl swooped low over the hedge in front of me. The long summer evenings on a bicycle must be the best way to discover Britain.

A short hop around the corner by Carlisle and you're in Scotland. Some nice folk in a farm let me stay in their kids' tent as I couldn't find anywhere to put my tent, due to the British Open being up the road at Turnberry. The good folk at Ardwell Farm fed me and sent me on my way to scuttle past the plaid tweeds of the golf tournament. There is a lot of golf on our isles. Even if you can't always see it, you can be riding quietly down some idyllic lane to hear the 'thwack' of club on ball. It's an odd game for odd people. Frankly, I'm a fan if only because it keeps all those people together and off the streets.

I rode around the beautiful Isle of Arran and stopped the night in Lochranza where I met Hans, a 71-year-old German who had been heading off on 800-mile cycle holidays each summer for the past 15 years or so. He was a great old boy, with a sparkle in his eye and some excellent biking tips. Like using a big filing elastic band around your front brake lever (stops a heavy bike rolling when you don't want it to). I spent a few hours nattering to Hans about his journeys and when I left him cycling off on to the Mull of Kintyre I noticed a little gift of one of his thick office elastic bands wrapped around my handlebar.

I don't know why, but the folk you meet on the road, even for just a short period, become your best friends, and there seems to be some kind of emotional bond that is hard to explain. I suppose in our day-to-day lives we meet so many folk almost in a businessy kind of way, but on the road you become much more sensitive and close to your emotions, and the people you spend time with become your best friends for that time. It's hard to explain, but it changes you and you carry this with you for a long time afterwards.

I met up with my wife, Harriet, three times on the journey; first in Glasgow, then in Berwick-upon-Tweed, and finally in Suffolk. They were the best and worst times of the journey. Best because it was so great to see her each time, and worst because for a day or so after she had gone home I felt so lonely.

One of the great things about a ride like this is that it's such a simple life. You get up, you eat, you ride, you meet inspiring people and make little films about them, you eat some more, you ride some more, you put up a tent, you sleep. Simple. And after a while you feel fitter and healthier and start to feel like you were made for this life.

Well after that high I should also tell you about the lows, which are mainly to do with wind, rain and cold. If you ride into the wind for days and weeks on end it is pretty sapping. There is nothing better than zipping along with the wind behind you, but riding into it on a heavy old bike is hard, hard work. Light rain is kind of refreshing; a wet road is nice to ride. But heavy rain over a day's riding is another thing. After an hour or two it starts seeping in past even the best wet-weather gear. It gets into your shoes and into your warm layers under your waterproofs. From then on, it's just unpleasant. Drying out in a tent is impossible, and I would often seek out a B&B to dry stuff. I would resort to setting a hairdryer propped up by books to dry my riding shoes and socks. I decided to bargain a bit with B&Bs as a kind of challenge, to see if I could get £5 or £10 knocked off. Only once (in Berwick-upon-Tweed) did I get a door slammed in my face when trying my bargaining technique. In contrast, there were B&Bs that refused to let me pay anything (this was more common in Ireland later) when they found out about my fundraising.

My big brother, Bob, has Parkinson's. He has always been a quiet, gentle sort of bloke and, since being diagnosed, I've never heard him complain; he just gets on with it. So it seemed entirely right that I should raise money for Parkinson's UK, the body that raises money for research. I have raised over £10,000 now but have never made a big thing of raising money, and only mentioned it if asked. But people are always generous, and it has astonished me how often someone would just give a passing cyclist £10 almost without question.

The west coast of Scotland is a mighty bicycle ride of over 1,000 miles and the map of each day's ride looks like some strange fjorded land. It felt completely new and alien to me. Even the names of places sound odd (well, to me anyway). This is a bit from a blog that I wrote in North West Scotland.

Managed to just make the 9.30 ferry across to Kilchoan and decided to get a long day in (with good weather forecast), the 20 miles on the south coast of Ardnamurchan is a great ride up to Salen and then another 40 miles north to Mallaig (where the ferry leaves for Mull). I am trying a little tactic of breaking the journeys into little 20-mile sections, with coffee and cake rewards. I've been working on eating more (as I lost a bit of weight in the first few weeks).

On Mull I met up for a cup of tea with Mike Carter, a journalist who was writing a piece each week for the *Observer*. Mike was doing the same journey by bicycle as me, except he was doing it anti-clockwise and had left his home in London a month or two before I set off. We met for another cup of tea almost two months later when we crossed paths again down in Falmouth.

One little excursion that I would really recommend is to the Orkneys. I took the Scrabster ferry to Stromness, which is a nice little town that reminded me of St Ives (though partly because the collection at the Pier Art Centre was mostly Cornish artists). Then I cycled over to the other town on Mainland, Kirkwall, where I set up camp.

On the ride to Kirkwall I came across and tagged onto a group about to go into Maeshowe, an ancient chambered cairn, an amazing 8-metre-high structure from 2700 BC. A nice aspect of the chamber itself is that a couple of Vikings broke into the chamber in about 1100 and graffitied the walls, telling stories of their heroics. On the midwinter solstice the setting sun aligns with the opening to illuminate the rear chamber of the cairn. This only happens on this one day.

The islands are treeless, just gentle low hills rising from the sea. I met a couple of Orkney strawback chair-makers, who told me that the tradition comes from the lack of wood. The wood for the structure of the chairs traditionally came from driftwood found on the beaches.

From Mainland I hopped on another ferry to Westray where I met up with two sisters who make clothes on this tiny little island. This would be the most northerly part of my journey. The birdlife is astounding on the Orkneys: there are Curlew all over the islands and on the ferries I saw Black Guillimots and Common Terns flitting by.

On Orkney I also saw the last of the Puffins to leave the islands for the summer. In fact, I was so excited about seeing a Puffin for the first time that I let go of my camera and watched it roll down the hill towards a cliff edge. Remarkably, someone lower down stopped and collected my camera as if it were rolling out of a scrum, walked up the hill and passed it back to me. I was already imagining the bit on the insurance form that asks how you lost your camera. To be honest I was a bit shocked, it was a very odd incident, and I'll never know the name of the lady who caught my camera so expertly. Suffice to say, I have been extra careful since.

I grew to really love the ferries all around our coast, proud and lovely vessels, always cheap for a cyclist, and always on time. It would be a time to relax and do nothing but look at some new coast or island appear, never quite knowing what was in store. There is something of the past, similar to seeing a steam train, about a ferry. Sometimes you would meet another cyclist, or someone would ask about my journey, or sometimes I would just sit, listen to some music and watch the sea.

On returning to the mainland from the Orkneys, I headed east. I had been in touch with Matt Hulse, a filmmaker, who was making a little film about Pilgrimage, which was Mark Cousins and Tilda Swinton's project to take a mobile cinema across Scotland for a week, showing classic films to villages and towns on the way. As it worked out, I met up with Pilgrimage on the last day in Nairn. I took in a film, the amazing *Sullivan's Travels*, and got to chat to Mark and Tilda to boot. There was a great atmosphere around the project and I think Nairn can be rightly proud of its famous daughter.

As often happens when I met inspiring people on this trip (which seemed to be most days), I left Nairn full of energy and enthusiasm for the next bit.

I loved those Bill Forsyth films of the '80s, *Local Hero* and *Gregory's Girl*. I looked out the little pub in Pennan where the pub in *Local Hero* was filmed. What I didn't know was that it is at the bottom of one of the steepest hills of the whole trip. The Pennan Inn with its famous phone box was for sale when I was there. I also stumbled across Ship Inn on the seafront in Banff, which is the bar that was used in the film. The climb out of Pennan, though, was the thing I will remember – so steep you worry that the front wheel would flip up at any moment.

I turned the corner and headed south for the first time down the east coast of Scotland. Everything speeds up now after the west coast – the roads are straighter and more direct. I headed around the beautiful Fife peninsula and into Edinburgh for a night. When you are alone on a road on pretty much any bit of British coastline you feel like you and your bicycle were made just for that moment. The opposite feels true, though, when you are heading into or out of many of our cities and towns. It feels like you are there at the mercy of the motor car and its owner's whims.

The Edinburgh festival was in full swing, so it was great to wander the city for a night. A lovely bloke called Mike Coulter put me up in the meeting room of his office in the city centre.

Leaving Edinburgh, I took a turn inland to avoid a busy A-road that hugs the coast and took a route across the Lammermuir Hills and out of Scotland into Northumberland. This bit of the coast is amazing. I nipped over the causeway to Lindisfarne, but in mid-August it's really crowded so I didn't hang around too long.

There was a great pub called The Ship in Newton-by-the-Sea. I enjoyed seeking out pubs and got really used to sitting with a pint listening to some local gossip, and it was always nice to head out and find a spot to pitch the tent after a pub visit.

After the beauty of Northumberland comes the industrial North East. There is a stretch from Tynemouth through Sunderland and into Hartlepool that feels like you are riding through 100 years of industry, ending up being carried on the brilliant transporter bridge over the Tees in Middlesbrough and then a ride out towards Redcar. Whitby was another dart in and out place because it was so crowded. There aren't the coal mines here any more, just memorials to them. But it still feels like the industrial heartland of the country.

I hopped onto a nice 25-mile stretch of old railway line which is now a cycle-track passing Robin Hood Bay. In Scarborough I stayed at Alison's, the first friend that I had stayed with since Cumbria. Alison gave me a grand tour of the town and she joined me on the road for a bit to celebrate the 3,000-mile mark. You get a lot of odd little shouts on the laden bike and a common one in the North East (often from people with a Jack Russell in tow) was 'Leavin' 'ome?'

Now I was heading south, I hopped inland a bit from Hull, as it seemed the roads were a little quieter on my route towards Mablethorpe. I was travelling east out of Louth and passing through a little village called Manby. Outside a little wooden house was a simple sign, 'Stickmaker'. Too good to pass by, I thought. I was greeted warmly by Jenny and Bill. The little soundslide that I made of Bill and his work tells its own story, but it was a lovely visit and I left with some rolls that Jenny had made. Bill is 72 and a countryman. He spends many hours fashioning walking and working sticks, selling them from his garage. He is modest about his own skills and preferred to ask about my journey. I felt afterwards that I would happily have ridden the 3,000-odd miles just to have met him and heard his story. I left after having bought a stick (which Bill posted home to Bristol).

Once past the Martin Parr world of Mablethorpe and Skegness, you take a left at Boston and into the flat lands of Norfolk and Suffolk. These are indeed beautiful huge landscapes.

I had bought a couple of tickets to see Wilco at the Troxy in London, and so cycled to Norwich and hopped on a train. I also took the opportunity to see my friends over at Innocent Drinks and do a little interview with the clothes designer Paul Smith, who is a massive cycle fan.

I quickly got back to the coast and continued south. By now I had an excellent beard and enjoyed being on the end of a road rage incident in Cromer, when someone shouted 'Beardie' at me for blocking his way.

South again. The weather turned wet and windy as I hopped over from Felixstowe into Harwich and Essex. This bit of the ride was like cycling through a bunch of Ian Dury lyrics, so places like Burnham-on-Crouch seemed familiar even though I'd never been there before. I liked Southend, but didn't enjoy the A-roads heading west past Canvey Island and it wasn't until I got to the Tilbury ferry that I began to feel like I belonged on the roads again. From Gravesend it was east and soon I was literally cycling through the laden orchards of Kent. I stayed in a brilliant little beach hut in Whitstable that belonged to Emrys, a friend of a friend. I loved Whitstable, a really nice little town to stay over in.

There was a lovely ride out of Whitstable where I cycled on the sea defences all the way to Margate and then round the corner to Dover, where, miraculously, you can see France just a short hop away. You can pretty much hug the coast here. Dungeness is amazing, like a frontier town in an old western film (albeit with nuclear power station), and I rode on to Rye, which is dead posh. To be honest I thought I had found a back way into Bath. I did, though, get a great deal in a little hotel that had a swimming pool and sauna, which was just amazing at the end of long hot day.

Thanks to Nicki and Vera, who contacted me through the website, I got a lovely welcome (and free nosh) at the C-side café in Bexhill-on-Sea, and also got to take a look at a Joseph Beuys exhibition in the brilliant De La Warr Pavilion, a modernist '30s gallery saved by the people of Bexhill from some development nightmare.

From here it was a short ride to Brighton, which I've always thought of as a kind of Bristol by the sea. Mostly because it's where people move from Hackney and Islington when their kids get to school age (well, they seem to go to either Bristol or Bath or Brighton).

I have this little gizmo on my bike that enabled me to upload my exact route each night to my website. It showed my distance, how much I climbed each day and my exact speed. One thing I quite liked about it is that it also showed where I went wrong and where I got lost. I quite liked it when I got lost, which is difficult to do when you are basically riding along the coast with the sea to your left. But it did happen a few times and it always was interesting. Like when I climbed a long hill on the Gower peninsula and found a spot with Skylarks all around where I could see the coast to the north and south. I also got lost a lot in towns and cities, often following cycle routes that petered out. Then I would ask a local. Actually I would normally ask a few locals and take a consensus view. I would often still end up on some grim by-pass or sometimes an ill-advised short cut across a field (which I did in Carlisle and ended up watching a Carlisle United training session for an hour).

Dorset is hilly, has a lot of military (I liked a sign that said 'sudden gunfire', wondering what other kind there was), and has very busy, scary roads on the coast.

Then into Devon and Cornwall. Lots more hills, Mostly they are in and out of fishing villages. Not complaining, though – each climb was worth it either for riding through a lovely little harbour town or village (like Fowey or Looe) or for a great cliff-top ride like Whitsand Bay west of Plymouth. I loved riding out along the Lizard peninsula to meet a fisherman called Nigel Legge who, I suppose, like a few fishermen, has several jobs including making lobster pots and selling his paintings. He also blagged a job as fishing adviser on *Ladies in Lavender*, a film made in the area. He fishes all morning, spends lunchtime in the pub and paints most days: not a bad life.

I hastily turned the corner at Land's End. Hasty only because both John O'Groats and Land's End are such odd places – they should both be beautiful isolated spots but have become sad little commercial oddities.

Two days before I finished the ride back in Bristol I stayed in this lovely little green metal house way down in a wooded valley in North Devon. It belongs to Rachel, a friend from Bath. I kept a note of what I wrote in the visitor's book in the house and it sums up quite well my feelings about this journey.

I arrived here after cycling 4,365 miles from Bristol. I have cycled the British coastline, leaving my home in Bristol on 21st June.

On my journey I have stayed in a tent a lot but also beach huts, a shepherd's hut, youth hostels, B&Bs, pubs, a caravan, with friends, with people who have offered to put me up. And finally here in this beautiful little wood and metal green house in the aptly named Welcombe on the north-west coast of Devon.

We live on an extraordinary amazing little island that we need to cherish and respect. We need to get in our cars less and be outside more, and most importantly we need to slow down a bit more in order to look around (and, by the way, a bike is a pretty perfect way to do that).

Oh, and one other thing: Britain is full of amazingly talented folk who are working in traditional and new crafts, from potters, to musicians, to painters, to people who work on the land or sea.

Thank you for letting me stay here. I am heading home to a party this Saturday, 3rd October, in Bristol after completing my journey around our little island.

Nick Hand

Electricity reading 9228

People say that an adventure changes you, and I'm sure that's true. For me, I found it particularly difficult to adjust back to my life as a graphic designer. I would be constantly looking out of the window at passing cyclists, wondering where they were going.

The following summer I continued my journey around the amazing coast of Ireland – no shortage of characters there. In total I have made over 100 little soundslides – each a tribute to the people of our coastline, the accents changing but the passion for their work and surroundings a constant. People tell me of exciting journeys in Europe or further afield, but for me I can't think of anywhere better to explore than our own beautiful islands. To look out from a saddle and study our funny quirky little ways. And to do it under your own power with the quiet slow pace of a bicycle is just perfect.

How to Tell the Difference between …

Grasshoppers and Crickets

One of the perennial problems for naturalists is how to tell the difference between crickets and grasshoppers. Whilst superficially these two groups of insects seem almost identical, with their long back legs, ability to jump long distances and habitat preferences, when you actually 'get your eye in' these two groups can be surprisingly easy to tell apart.

If you've ever wondered about the difference between grasshoppers and crickets then you're about to discover a few simple ways that will let you tell them apart with ease.

Antennae

Possibly the quickest and easiest way to tell a grasshopper from a cricket is by taking a look at the antennae. In grasshoppers these tend to be short and sticking out in front of the head, whilst in crickets these are normally very long indeed – sometimes as long as the insect – and are often swept back along the body, though they may be waved about in the air.

Body Shape

Grasshoppers typically have a far longer, thinner, more 'aerodynamic' body shape than crickets, which are typically far more rounded in shape.

Time of Day

When it comes to the chirping song of these two similar groups of insects, they will normally sing at different times of the day. You're most likely to hear grasshoppers calling during the day whilst crickets are the likely culprit if you hear noise later on in the day and during the evening.

Habitat

Whilst grasshoppers and crickets both seem to like wild, grassy areas there are often subtle differences between their habitat choices. Grasshoppers favour short, tussocky grassland where they can climb to the top of stems to sun themselves, whilst I tend to find crickets far more often in longer grass, or even on the leaves of bushes and trees where grasshoppers are seldom seen.

Living on a
Remote Island

Sarah Boden

I live on an island called Eigg. It's one of the smaller dots off Scotland's west shoulder which speckle the Atlantic like bits of floating dandruff. The looming profile of the Sgurr, its only peak, catches your eye on the horizon after a five-hour run on the West Highland line. As it rattles around tight corners, the toolbox-on-wheels that is the two-carriage train from Glasgow sloshes ripples into your cup of oily trolley tea. Positioned within sight but not easy reach, Eigg has a bewitching allure. Resplendent against a wash of watery sunlight or under a smirr of rainclouds, it always makes my heart sing a little. The final leg of the journey is an hour-long boat ride across the waters of the Minch. On a bad day, as waves spray your face with brine and tourists splatter the deck with vomit, the 15 miles feel interminably longer.

About 87 people live here. The same number that fills a London rush-hour double-decker. From crofters to hippies, doctors to dropouts, farmers to teachers. They're just more practical than your typical mainlander. Eigg is not a big place. You can walk from end to end in a few hours. Islanders live in modest houses scattered between rocks and tufty hillocks. There is a shop that you can pace round in ten steps, a ceilidh hall and a tearoom that doubles as a bar come the weekend. Rounds of 'red cans', aka McEwen's Export, are usually kept company by large drams. You can buy drink on tick and bad hangovers are later shadowed by a dry-mouthed queasiness on eyeballing your month-end bar bill.

In winter the Troon-built steel tub the MV *Loch Nevis* calls four times a week. People bustle down to the pier to collect their letters, food orders, animal feed and an assortment of heavily wrapped, sometimes oddly shaped parcels. Every so often a cargo boat called the *Spanish John* arrives with coal, red diesel and bales of hay that are dragged from the pier with dilapidated tractors or tied to van roofs. These seemingly prosaic occasions are the social lubricant which keeps islanders from lone-wolf seclusion. A welcome chance to stand and blether in the comfort of company.

I grew up here as a young child, only returning last year to take on the tenancy of my uncle's 2,000-acre hill farm with my family. My hands are freshly calloused and I spend each day in waterproof bib and brace overalls but it feels like an honest day's work. After eight years of dissolute London living, it took a few months to rid myself of city jitters. Day-to-day, when I'm chasing a recalcitrant tup or trying not to get trampled by hungry cows, I'm unmindful of my surroundings. When I pause for breath and raise my eyes, I can't help but drink in the scenery with a covetous thirst.

Nature's stark elegance is always a restorative draught. There's something in the dramatic up-thrust of the mountains and the uninterrupted ocean horizon that infects you with a sense of amplified emotion. The rhythms of the day are more leisurely but, as you mark the rise of the tide and the sun's progress across the sky, you're more aware of them. Cloud formations, the height of the sun and the wind direction are caught in the sea's reflective surface, so the scenery is a constantly changing tableau.

Surveying the mainland peaks, your sense of isolation is amplified by the expanse of water encircling the island like a deep moat. Silver quartz beaches are backed by giant boulders hewed into striking shapes by fierce winds and Atlantic waves. Offshore shags stand with their wings stretched like sentinels on black, jagged rocks, and seals peer from the water with dark, watchful eyes. Some days, the sea is as smooth and flat as a lily pond and the air so still that the chugging progress of a passing fishing boat carries for miles. When the autumn equinox arrives in late September, the storms leave you slack-jawed at nature's savage strength. Waterfalls are blown vertical, trees stripped of their leaves in a night and garden plants flattened like wilted spinach.

The summer brings fragrant carpets of wild flowers: harebells, grass-of-parnassus, bog asphodel, wild thyme and orchids. In silent braes and meadows that were once crofting settlements, you stumble over the walls of abandoned stone houses sleeping under a blanket of turf and lichen. Often you struggle to paw a path through dense thickets of encroaching bracken. The ground undulates with the gentle curves of old lazy beds. Crofters lugged creels of seaweed from the shore to pile onto inaccessible hillsides and grow potatoes in the acid soil. These evocations of a recent, back-breaking human past lend a sometimes eerie, occasionally comforting feeling to your meanders.

The retreat of the native islanders, despite the grasp that this place had on them, is confirmation of how tough life once was on Eigg. It's still difficult to earn a living here. Most people turn their hand to several jobs: picking whelks in the winter; selling eggs and vegetables; shooting rabbits and cleaning holiday houses. The thing is, despite its unspoilt beauty, remote idylls like this are soulless without people. In the popular imagination islands are synonymous with escape but you don't 'opt out' by moving to an island, you tie yourself in to a collective psyche, whether you like it or not.

The notion of living in a community – a hazy and remote conceit when I lived in London – is a reality. Small acts of kindness make a difference; neighbours can be called on for a wee session or a cup of tea; most islanders, young and old, turn up to parties at the wooden ceilidh hall. True enough, living cheek-by-jowl, people think they have the measure of each other. Their closeness is a solace and an awful thing. It gives you a sense of security: to leave your car with the keys in the ignition; to pick up your jumper where you left it on a soused Friday night; and most importantly, to know that people will help if you ask.

When left to do what you fancy for too long, however, it is easy to become calcified. If you haven't left the island for a while, it feels as if your world is shrinking. The same topics of discussion crop up ad infinitum; you know there's no one you vaguely fancy on the island, never mind want to shag (but on some unfortunate occasion you probably will); and it is a certainty that somebody is keeping half an eye on what you're up to. In fact, if you're overly bothered by what people think, then islands are not for you. You can't avoid a sour-faced character who wants to drop-kick you off a cliff when you're on a single-track road. If your life is lacking in gossip-worthy escapades then it'll get made up, often with a mean comic twist. An islander returning from unspecified medical treatment, it was speculated, had gone away for the removal of in-grown arse hairs.

Like every island Eigg attracts dreamers. The seed is planted by romanticised books, articles or some TV adventurer in expensive waterproofs bellowing about the elemental majesty of the Hebrides. All the well-worn themes are true enough: you can get back to nature, throw off the shackles of suburban living, immerse yourself in contemplative silence. But a simpler life doesn't mean you can renounce responsibility. Typically, wide-eyed new arrivals trying to escape spiritual torpor find that the cause of their misery is themselves. Without distractions, you have to stare yourself in the face, and it can be a comfortless experience. There's nothing to stir melancholy like a short winter's day clamped under a grey sky, surrounded by a vicious sea. Some days you can't even leave the house. You step outside the front door only to be pinned to the wall by the wind like a paper doll. These types usually leave suddenly, perhaps afraid that their resolve will waver, or maybe they can't get away fast enough. For now, it suits me just fine.

Radnorshire Annual

Richard King

For the last ten years my wife and I have lived in Powys, mid Wales. Powys is divided into three shires: Brecknockshire, Radnorshire and Montgomeryshire. The county's eastern border runs along The Marches with Shropshire and Herefordshire, so by the 18th century the county was largely anglicised. As someone who regularly cries while singing the national anthem, 'Hen Wlad Fy Nhadau', at the Millennium Stadium, I was astonished to hear it sung in English by some of our older neighbours when we first moved here. Our home is in Radnorshire, a few hundred yards from the banks of the River Wye, a natural divide between Radnorshire and Brecknockshire.

Radnorshire suffers from the least light pollution in Britain, and to widespread local disbelief Powys recently came top in a survey of national happiness. Powys is Wales' largest county but has its smallest population. Very rarely does a day go by when I don't stop in wonder at the fact we are able to live here, in such a stimulating rural wilderness. Given the area's sense of isolation, it's perhaps unsurprising that the prejudices often associated with the narrowest of countryside thinking can be sometimes overheard; a reminder, along with the closing of Post Offices, shops and pubs, that this is no broadsheet idyll.

We live among a community of hill farmers whose white stone farmhouses and out-buildings illuminate the endless patchwork of rolling green fields that stretch far into the horizon across the Cambrian Mountains. Our first home here was a smallholder's cottage, rented to us by a sheep farmer on the understanding that it was still part of a working farm environment. This often meant opening and shutting gates, running after wayward lambs and negotiating the herd with occasionally witless sheepdogs more interested in nipping the lambs' ankles than organising their route. Our life moves to the rhythms of farming accordingly: lambing in the spring, shearing in the summer, market in the early autumn and then, in October, in the last of the sunshine, the tups are introduced into the fields with the ewes and the cycle begins again.

On a warm spring day, the sight of the first-born lambs running deliriously across the fields together makes the endless grey rain of winter a distant memory. A walk along the riverbank a few weeks later, knee deep in wild garlic, watching the heron, curlew and kingfisher making the river their own is more than compensation for the hour-long drive to the nearest train station.

The course of our year follows such moments. Everyone, wherever they are, has their own set of signposts for the progress of the year, a combination of habit, family traditions and superstition.

I.

Listen, now, verse should be as natural
As the small tuber that feeds on muck
And grows slowly from obtuse soil
To the white flower of immortal beauty.

R.S. Thomas, 'Poetry for Supper'

The process of chitting potatoes is one we are all familiar with from childhood – potatoes exposed to the light start to sprout thin new stems of growth. Our potatoes are, eventually, after we have given ourselves interminable reminders, placed on a windowsill at the end of January and left to slowly bud. In the meantime the muck has been dug into the obtuse soil. The thick uneven clods usually spend part of the winter covered in snow; then a layer of impenetrable frost, so thick it looks almost blue in the thin winter sunlight, hardens the ground. The manure combines with the soil as it melts, becoming food for the worms that under the watchful eye of robins drag the clods back down beneath the surface.

Indoors, the sprouting potatoes look pale and fragile, their upward progress echoed outside by the snowdrops pushing through the grass to announce the end of winter. The first of March is St David's Day, upon which we are meant, as a country, to awaken to the sight of daffodils, their golden trumpet heads a symbolic chorus of a shared national identity. Daffodils here resist such convention by flowering later in the month, magnificently lining the B-road hedgerows in crowds of yellow. The bards have long argued that a sense of place is more fundamental than patriotism.

By mid-March the potato trenches are dug and filled with the first grass cuttings of the year, along with any spare newspaper that has survived the endless re-lighting of the wood burner. Both paper and grass are soaked and raked in, a luxury new home for the spuds, whose etymology in the word spade reflects the labour-intensive process of eating your own. The grass cuttings indicate that the soil is warm enough to receive the crop, often to the sound of newborn lambs. Days old and encountering the outside world for the first time, the lambs sound optimistic yet terrified, their legs so thin and long in comparison to the rest of their bodies that they involuntarily bounce on the spot. Covering over the potatoes means soil up to the elbows and dark brown fingernails for the first time in months. The farmer's hands are similarly stained and bloodied from hours spent lambing through the night, his role endlessly shifting from midwife to vet, and occasionally to undertaker.

2.

The half-hardy annuals' seeds sown in early spring are next on the windowsills, leaving a trail of compost and water damage on the cracking paint. Growing annual flowers ensures that over time you discover a new language, not the botanical Latin of *Calendula officinalis* (Marigold), *Lathyrus odoratus* (Sweet Pea) or *Leucanthemum vulgare* (Oxeye daisy) but the technical terms for turning seedlings into flowers: pinching-out, pricking-out, potting-on; start using these phrases and it's possible to will yourself into having at least the pretence of green fingers. Though planted out in milder parts of the country at the beginning of May, our annuals stay in their pots, slowly acclimatising to the wind, away from the risk of frost until Whitsun.

Over the last few years, at some point over the weekend, we have listened to Larkin reading 'The Whitsun Weddings'. Larkin is a poet who, with a degree of justification, has not settled well in the hearts of either his readers or the wider public. His reputation has been posthumously revised thanks to the publication of his letters that revealed a darker, harsher, more troubled soul than the merely morose one he projected.

Whatever your thoughts of the letters, 'The Whitsun Weddings' is a remarkable poem about this country. A train journey starting in Hull and ending in London takes in cattle, 'canals with floatings of industrial froth', suburbs, cricket, sighs and smut, before ending with the line 'Sent out of sight, somewhere becoming rain', and telling us more, in the ordinariness of it all, about the spirit running through the United Kingdom than any poster or mug suggesting you Keep Calm and Carry On.

Listening to Larkin's voice at Whitsun, when the hours and daylight are racing along at a pace that seemed inconceivable at the start of the year, is an act of time travel. We share a fixed moment on the calendar with the poet, one that reveals the similarities and differences of his time and ours, the past and present sharing a railway carriage together.

Once the annuals are planted out some of the early flowering varieties are starting to fade. Peonies have deep red flowers in the early spring, a vivid contrast to the greens and yellows everywhere else. By June the peony flowers are starting to fall, a sign, according to one of our neighbours, that shearing time has arrived.

Waiting their turn under the razor the lambs are growing fast and independent, and away from their mothers are much more vulnerable. During summer a caged rook is placed in the fields among the ewes and lambs. The rook, frustrated at being captive, lets out a series of distinct and strange-sounding cries. Recognising the cry of a trapped and agitated bird, other rooks stay well away. They can often be seen hopping sinisterly among the sheep, a sharp black presence waiting for a lamb to become isolated before launching a few feet into the wind, then swooping down to duly peck out its eye. The sight of a young dead lamb, the drained blood drying around its eye sockets, is not easy to forget. No wonder Ted Hughes spent long hours in contemplation of our mortality and the relationship between lambs, crows, earth, blood and sky.

3.

On Midsummer's eve we have often taken advantage of the length of daylight by walking in Cwm Elan, the Elan Valley. Sometimes known as the desert of Wales, Elan Valley has an extraordinary atmosphere. At the height of summer its barren roads are visible by moonlight, as is its vast liquid landmass of water. A network of Victorian dams and reservoirs, a huge area over seventy miles square, the valley was flooded by an Act of Parliament at the end of the 19th century in order to provide Birmingham, then a sickly city, with a fresh water supply. The valley's occupants were forcibly removed while only the landowners, a fraction of the population, were offered compensation. There are moments, when walking in the beauty of the Elan, that one senses what was lost both physically and spiritually by turning a wilderness into a utility. Over a century later, the marvels of Victorian engineering and the glass and copper elegance of the domes and roofs of the dam buildings are now as astonishing as the vandalism that allowed them to be built. Cwm Elan is still magnificently wild, but its drama, or perhaps its tragedy, is now man-made.

As the summer starts to fade Cwm Elan has another reason for a visit. Mushrooms abound on its deciduous paths: chicken of the woods, parasols, blewits and field mushrooms are all within a ten-minute walk on the right trail. If your luck is in there will be ceps among the beech and oak trees, and where there are ceps there will almost certainly be found, for the truly adventurous, fly agaric. I often wonder why there hasn't been a record label or band called Fly Agaric; the name alone would guarantee you an audience at a certain sort of music festival. For about three years we have had wet summers followed by unseasonal autumn heat waves, a mycologist's nightmare. Last year I spoke to a local expert who confided that he hadn't seen a mushroom for three years. He may have been exaggerating; we drank some of his homemade cider and it certainly tasted fungal.

With the autumn comes change; the lambs are separated from their mothers and prepared for market. This involves them being given a 'bloom dip', which in the words of one of our neighbours is 'a bloody stupid caper'. More or less a shampoo and set for sheep, a bloom dip is a foul-smelling routine which results in the lambs looking good, i.e. slightly bigger, for market. No farmer we know wants to waste time or money doing it, but no one dares break ranks and have their stock look smaller – and therefore cheaper – than the competition once the flock is at market.

Separated by two or three gates and several acres for the first time since birth, the ewes and lambs nevertheless hear one another and cry out accordingly, a sound that has kept us awake through the night more than once. The lambs are loaded up into the trailers and peace descends, with just a hint of eeriness in the silence. The feeling of being under-prepared for the winter is acute. There is never quite enough wood, some winter crops have gone to seed too early because of the mild weather and we have forgotten to sow anything to replace them; then comes the dark, and life moves inside.

4.

In Wales, in my family and I'm sure many others, the short-est day is known as Cam Ceiliog. Like much of the language, and the nation as a whole, especially our fly halves, it makes sense when considered poetically. Roughly translated, Cam Ceiliog is the length of a cockerel's step. It describes the distance by which we can see the daylight start to extend as we walk away from the winter's depths. From this moment every day grows a little, and the light returns, by the length of a cockerel's footstep. Cam Ceiliog holds an intangibility to stir the heart. We are just, now, on this shortest of days, at what T.S. Eliot called 'the still point of the turning world'.

Garlic, that humble elixir for the winter grey, was tradi-tionally planted on Midwinter's day and harvested six months later on Midsummer morning. Such horticultural equilibrium turns gardening into alchemy. Though a long way off, Midsummer in all its dancing colour, whether late into the evening or round the back of a tent somewhere in the quickening dawn, is where the mirror is now headed.

Cam Ceiliog suggests a moment of quiet reflection. There is much celebration and cutting loose to come in the next week or so, but Cam Ceiliog is an echo chamber, a wisp of a day that vanishes just as soon as it appears. A day to wander around in your mind's interior, just a few moments of thought and the shortest day is done. I think of it as a lambent beacon in the dark, a sign to raise a glass and make a quiet toast to your inner Beltane.

In the weeks ahead, if you find yourself sloughing through the back end of winter, and its tendency to immovable gloom – pace yourself. Cam Ceiliog has marked a path through midwinter. The daylight is coming. One step at a time.

Waterfall Staircase

August 1958

A. Harry Griffin

One of the few things worth doing in the Lake District on a really wet day – a clarty day, we would call it – is looking at waterfalls. An even better thing, if you are of the adventurous type or just plain stupid, depending on how you view things, is to climb one. The argument is that having decided to go out on the fells and get wet (without seeing any scenery), one might as well do the job properly just for the fun of it, and have a bit of excitement thrown in. Some routes up Lake District crags are delightfully described in the books as 'an ideal wet weather climb'; the one we tackled the other day was summed up by 'the greater the volume of water, the greater the difficulty and interest'. The one merit of this particular route was that one became drenched through to the skin immediately after starting, thus avoiding the unpleasant ordeal of getting wet through by degrees. Being really wet through is no discomfort, they say, provided one keeps moving. The climbing difficulties proved to be slight, but communications were trying. Because of the thunder and the crash of the pounding water it was impossible to hear oneself speak, let alone the other, and when out of sight of each other with the rope churning in the torrent we savoured, through the spray, the 'interest' mentioned in the guidebook.